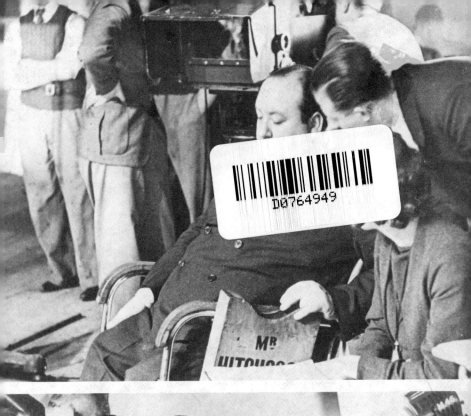

THE LADY VANISHES

directed by
ALFRED HITCHCOCK

screenplay by
Frank Launder and Sidney Gilliat,
From the novel THE WHEEL SPINS
by Ethel Lina White

Lorrimer Publishing

CONTENTS

ACKNOWLEDGEMENTS

Our thanks are due to Cyril Howard of Pinewood Studios for making the publication of this screenplay possible, to the British Film Institute for its research facilities and photographic stills, and especially to Elaine Crowther for preparing this continuity from the release script and the film itself.

INTRODUCTION
by Andrew Sinclair

The Lady Vanishes was made in 1938 at a time of suspended disbelief and uneasy diplomacy in Europe. The British Prime Minister, Neville Chamberlain, had arranged 'a peace in our time' with Hitler at Munich, a peace that few expected to last for long. Parts of Czechoslovakia had been sacrificed to German expansion. Poland was threatened in the same way. A Second World War seemed imminent because of plots and claims and subterfuges in Central Europe. Alfred Hitchcock chose to film a novel, *The Wheel Spins*, by Ethel Lina White: it was set on a train making its way through that troubled region, menaced by conflict, bubbling with intrigue.

Although *The Lady Vanishes* chose wit and suspense rather than a political message, its relevance as well as the brilliance of its making led to instant acclaim, particularly in America, where it won the New York Critics Award. Both Orson Welles and James Thurber saw it a dozen times, while the acute Howard Barnes compared Hitchcock's craftsmanship with a Cezanne canvas or a Stravinsky score. Along with *The Thirty-Nine Steps*, this film remains the most popular of the Hitchcock films made in Britain, both for its mastery of technique and lightness of touch.

It was filmed on a small budget on a ninety-foot stage in Islington. There was no exterior shooting: Hitchcock did marvels with miniatures, rear projection and glass shots. It was Michael Redgrave's first film role: Margaret Lockwood had never worked with Hitchcock before. 'He never really mixed with the actors,' she recalled. 'He knew exactly what he wanted, where the camera had to be set up. So you did what he wanted, that was it! I could speak for hours with Carol Reed, but Hitch . . . ' [*SEE*

1

At Hitchcock's direction, the two screenwriters, Frank Launder and Sidney Gilliat, made significant changes from the novel. The hero Gilbert was metamorphosed from a dam engineer to a collector of folk music. A banker became a magician in order to introduce the sequence of the trick cabinet and the poster of the Vanishing Lady. Miss Froy was transposed from a gullible governess into a British secret agent, while Hitchcock made his purpose clear in the lines explaining her name, Froy, not Freud. 'It rhymes with joy.' Hitchcock intended to make a thriller of joyous action, not of psychological motivation. The lady vanishes, she does not withdraw into herself.

Various themes thread the script, the theme of families – true and false – against traitors and nations: the theme of unwilling commitment because of necessity: the theme of misunderstanding through language: and the theme of identity, whether a person exists or does not.

The whole of an identity, at one moment, appears an illusion, a vanishing trick. Appearances are not realities. But Hitchcock does not labour over philosophy or significance. He conjures with the art of film.

After a witty introduction in the snow-bound resort hotel, Hitchcock builds suspense on suspense, deception on revelation, like a maestro playing the fifty-two card trick. With the heroine, we cannot believe the evidence of her eyes. Miss Froy's handwriting on the window, the only surety of her existence, disappears like the Uncertainty Principle on the moment of its discovery. The bandaged patient may contain the vanished lady, or a corpse, or anyone. As for the nun in high heels, she is the stuff of dream as well as deception. And the illusion of the moving train itself, although filmed in a small studio, hustles us towards an excitement, a denouement, and explosions of laughter to relieve the suspense. *The Lady Vanishes* is Hitchcock at his most worldly and assured. Yet beneath the entertainment, there is the menace of a Europe about to plunge into the horror of war.

CAST

Margaret Lockwood	Iris Henderson
Michael Redgrave	Gilbert Redman
Paul Lukas	Dr. Hartz
Dame May Whitty	Miss Froy
Cecil Parker	Eric Todhunter
Linden Travers	Margaret
Mary Clare	Baroness
Naunton Wayne	Caldicott
Basil Radford	Charters
Emile Boreo	Manager
Googie Withers	Blanche
Philip Leaver	Doppo
Catherine Lacey	Nun
Charles Oliver	Officer
Sally Stewart	Julie
Zelma Vas Dias	Signora Doppo
Josephine Wilson	Madame Kummer
Kathleen Tremaine	Anna

CREDITS

Producer	Edward Black
Director	Alfred Hitchcock
from the novel "The Wheel Spins" by	Ethel Lina White
Screenplay	Frank Launder, Sidney Gilliat
Continuity	Alma Reville
Photography	Jack Cock
Assistant cameraman	Leo Harris
Location photography	Jack Parry, Maurice Oakley
Music by	Cecil Milner
Musical Director	Louis Levy
Editors	Alfred Roome
	R.E. Dearing
Art Director	Alec Vetchinsky
Assisted by	Maurice Carter, Albert Jullion
Sound recordist	Sidney Wiles

NOTE: The Bandrieken spoken throughout the film is a fictitious language. The English translations are put down to convey the meaning of the sequence.

THE LADY VANISHES

The film opens with an exterior shot of snow-capped mountains over which the titles are superimposed.
Camera tracks and pans down from the peaks into the village and on to an hotel.
The hotel foyer is packed with travellers. MISS FROY *passes through, depositing her key with* BORIS, *the hotel manager, who is standing behind the reception desk.* CALDICOTT *and* CHARTERS *impatiently wait in the foyer, not knowing what is going on. Everyone is talking rapidly and loudly; it is late afternoon.*
BORIS *is talking into the telephone.*

BORIS: 'Allo. Prosto. Prosto. (Hallo. Quickly. Quickly). Signorina. Signore.
Se la moledicate le trena bianga de meno parpicheri, commi radiostroni del maruma ha! ha! Mesdames, Messier, le train va arrive seulment de matin (Hallo . . . hallo . . . quickly . . . quickly. The train is held up until tomorrow. What a rush for rooms there's going to be . . . Ladies and gentlemen, the train will not leave until tomorrow morning.)

CALDICOTT: What's all this fuss about, Charters?

CHARTERS: Hanged if I know.

BORIS: Mein Darmen unt Herron. Bitterscheoun reaistronen . . . (My dear ladies and gentlemen . . . will you please register now).

The reception desk becomes crowded with travellers.
CHARTERS *and* CALDICOTT *look on bemused.*

BORIS: Dankerschern (Thank you very much). Dankerschern. Ladies and gentlemen, I'm very sorry the train is a little bit uphold, and if you wish to stay in my hotel

. . . you will have to register immediately.

CHARTERS: Why the deuce didn't he say so in the first place?

They make for the reception desk. BORIS *leaves.*
Outside the hotel BORIS *meets* IRIS, BLANCHE, *and* JULIE *about to enter. They are dressed in hill-walking clothing and are tired. He stops them on the hotel steps.*

BORIS: How do you do, Miss Henderson. How do you do, ladies. It is a great honour to have you with us again.

IRIS: It's nice to see you too, Boris. You haven't changed a bit since last Friday.

BLANCHE: Mm . . . I see you haven't shaved either.

JULIE: Is everything ready?

BORIS: Everything is ready. I didn't change anything.

IRIS: Not even the sheets, we know. Lead on, Boris.

BORIS: You see, I didn't expect you to come so quickly.

IRIS: Well, our legs gave out on us. We had to do the last lap in a farm cart.

BORIS: Oh!

BLANCHE: I see we've got company. Don't tell me Cooks are running cheap tours here.

IRIS: What is it, Boris?

BORIS: The havelunch!

JULIE: Have a lunch?

IRIS: Avalanche, Boris. Avalanche.

BORIS: You see, in the spring, we've got many avalanches. You know, the snow go like that. Boom! And everything disappears. Even trains disappear under the avalanche.

IRIS: But I'm going home tomorrow. How long before they dig it out?

6

BORIS: By morning. It's lucky for you you can leave by this train, instead of your own. How did you said it? It's a bad wind that blow nowhere no good.

BLANCHE: And talking of wind, we haven't eaten since dawn.

IRIS: Serve us some supper, Boris, in our room.

JULIE: I could eat a horse.

IRIS: Don't put ideas into his head. Er . . . some chicken, Boris, and a magnum of champagne.

They all enter the hotel and we see CALDICOTT, CHARTERS *and the travellers still crowded in to the foyer.*

IRIS *off:* And make it snappy.

BLANCHE *off:* Bandrika may have a Dictator . . .

IRIS, BLANCHE, JULIE *and* BORIS *come back into shot.*

BLANCHE: . . . but tonight we're painting it red.

The action cuts to the foyer. We see a medium-length camera shot of CALDICOTT *and* CHARTERS *surrounded by travellers.*

CHARTERS: Meanwhile, we have to stand here cooling our heels, I suppose, eh? Confounded impudence.

CALDICOTT: Third rate country. What do you expect?

CHARTERS: Wonder who all those women were?

CALDICOTT: Probably Americans, I should think. You know, almighty dollar, old man.

CHARTERS: Oh, well, I suppose we'll have to wait here. If only we hadn't missed that train at Budapest.

CALDICOTT: I don't want to rub it in, but if you hadn't insisted on standing up until they'd finished their National Anthem . . .

CHARTERS: Yes, but you must show respect, Caldicott. If I'd known it was going to last twenty minutes . . .

7

CALDICOTT: Well, it's always been my contention that the Hungarian Rhapsody is not their National Anthem. In any case, we were the only two standing.

CHARTERS: That's true.

CALDICOTT: Well, I suppose we shall be in time after all.

CHARTERS: I doubt it. That last report was pretty ghastly, do you remember? England on the brink.

CALDICOTT: Yes, but that's newspaper sensationalism. The old country's been in some tight corners before.

CHARTERS: Looks pretty black. I mean, even if we get away first thing tomorrow morning, there's still the connection at Basle. We'll probably be hours.

CALDICOTT: Mm . . . that's true.

CHARTERS: Somebody surely can help us. Oh, sir! Do you happen to know what time the train leaves Basle for England?

Pan to include BENNING.

BENNING: Ich sprekker kein Englisch (I don't speak English).

CHARTERS: Oh, really! The fellow doesn't speak English.

The camera has moved to a long shot of BORIS *on the telephone.*

BORIS *into phone*: 'Allo . . . Alex . . . Na Kruska natra trappa par kartiska, yah denecatisca champagne Miss Henderson. Griska, Griska, oi veys mille (Hallo, Alex . . . Put everything else aside and take some chicken and a magnum of champagne to Miss Henderson).

BORIS *comes off the telephone and turns to face the travellers, all of whom wish to have some accommodation. A* WOMAN *breaks into a torrent of rapid French saying she wants a double room with a bath. Camera pans onto* CALDICOTT *and* CHARTERS, *who are reading a railway timetable beside the reception desk.*

CHARTERS: Here's one leaves Basle, twenty-one twenty.

CALDICOTT: Twenty-one twenty?

CHARTERS: Yes.

CALDICOTT: Twenty, twenty. Twelve from twenty.

Cut back to the hotel reception desk where BORIS *is being harrassed by visitors.*

BORIS: I regret, sir, there is only left two single rooms in front, or a little double room at the back.

TODHUNTER: We'll, er . . . take the two singles.

BORIS: Very well, sir. Here is . . . Thank you.

TODHUNTER *snatches the key and he and* "MRS." TODHUNTER *move away from the reception desk.*

"MRS." TODHUNTER: At least you might have asked me which I preferred.

TODHUNTER: My dear, a small double room at the back in a place like this . . .

"MRS." TODHUNTER: You weren't so particular in Paris last autumn.

TODHUNTER: It was quite different then. The Exhibition was at its height.

"MRS." TODHUNTER: I realise that now. There's no need to rub it in.

CALDICOTT *and* CHARTERS *finally reach the front of the queue in front of the reception desk.*

CALDICOTT: We want a private suite with a bath.

CHARTERS: Facing the mountains.

CALDICOTT: And with a shower, of course.

CHARTERS: Hot and cold.

CALDICOTT: And a private thingummy, if you've got one.

BORIS: Well, I'm sorry, gentlemen, the only thing I've got is the maid's room.

CALDICOTT: Maid's room!

CHARTERS: What's that?

BORIS: Well, I'm sorry. The whole hotel is packed. Jammed to the sky.

CALDICOTT: But that's impossible. We haven't fixed up yet.

CHARTERS: Hang it all, you can't expect to put the two of us up in the maid's room.

BORIS: Well, don't get excited, I'll remove the maid out.

CHARTERS: I should think so. What? What are you talking about?

CALDICOTT: Look here, I think I'd sooner sleep on the train.

BORIS: There is no 'eating in the train.

CALDICOTT: No eating on the train?

BORIS: Yes, I mean heating. Brrr.

CALDICOTT: Oh, there's no heating on the train.

CHARTERS: That's awkward. All right, we'll take it.

BORIS: Just a minute, on one condition. You have to have the maid come to your room, er . . . remove her wardrobe.

As CHARTERS, CALDICOTT *and* BORIS *stand looking at one another,* ANNA *comes into the shot.*

BORIS: Anna! She's a good girl, and I don't want to lose her. La cracka des tequa le freita del la castilla aratita la couta heh (Will it be all right for those two gentlemen to have your room)?

ANNA *smiles. The camera cuts rapidly between* ANNA *and* CHARTERS *and* CALDICOTT *and back again.*

CHARTERS: We'd better go and dress.

CALDICOTT: Rather primitive humour, I thought.

CHARTERS: Grown-up children, you know. That was rather an awkward situation, over that girl.

CALDICOTT: Pity he couldn't have given us one each.

CHARTERS: Eh?

CALDICOTT: I mean a room apiece.

CHARTERS: Oh!

> CHARTERS *and* CALDICOTT *ascend the stairs. We cut to the interior of* IRIS'S *bedroom. There is a long shot of* JULIE *and* BLANCHE. IRIS *is standing on a table; she is in her lingerie.*

IRIS: I, Iris Matilda Henderson. A spinster of no particular parish, do hereby solemnly renounce my maidenly past . . .

> *The camera cuts from* IRIS *to* RUDOLPH, *the waiter, entering with a tray. His face registers surprise at* IRIS *on the table. We focus on* RUDOLPH *as he tries to place the contents of the tray on the table that* IRIS *is on, and his reactions to* IRIS'S *legs. The camera cuts between his face and* IRIS'S *legs and the faces of* BLANCHE *and* JULIE.

IRIS *off:* . . . and do declare that on Thursday next, the twenty-sixth inst., being in my right mind, I shall take the veil . . . and the orange blossom . . . and change my name to Lady Charles . . .

> RUDOLPH *stares at* IRIS'S *legs in front of him.*

IRIS *off:* Fotheringail.

BLANCHE *off:* Can't you get him to change his name instead?

JULIE *off:* The only thing I like about him is his moustache.

> *We cut to a medium camera shot of* IRIS *still on the table.*

11

IRIS: You're a couple of cynics. I'm very fond of him.

We see IRIS'S *legs again and* RUDOLPH'S *face.*

BLANCHE *off:* Well, I'm fond of rabbits, but they have to be kept down.

IRIS *off:* Rudolph, give me a hand.

RUDOLPH *helps* IRIS *down from the table.*

BLANCHE: Have you ever read about that little thing called love?

JULIE: It used to be very popular.

IRIS: Child, the carpet is already laid at St. George's, Hanover Square, and Father is simply aching to have a coat of arms on the jam label.

JULIE: To Iris, and the happy days she's leaving behind.

BLANCHE: And the blue-blooded cheque-chaser she's dashing to London to marry.

JULIE: The blue-blooded cheque-chaser.

IRIS: I've no regrets. I've been everywhere and done everything. I've eaten caviare at Cannes, sausage rolls at the dogs. I've played Baccarat at Biarritz, and darts with the rural dean. What is there left for me but marriage?

We cut to the corridor of the hotel. RUDOLPH *is closing the girls' bedroom door as* ANNA *ascends the stairs to the landing. She joins him.*

ANNA: Ques embraces sedara enduro on-train stirrana (This is a nice thing having to give up one's own bedroom to passengers on the train).

RUDOLPH: Craman vin cam fin satto (Who is going in to your room)?

ANNA: En fun das l'englistos (Two Englishmen).

RUDOLPH: L'englistos (Englishmen)?

ANNA: Griska (That's right).

12

We are in ANNA'S *bedroom.* CALDICOTT *and* CHARTERS *are dressing for dinner.*

CHARTERS: It's this hanging about that gets me. If only we knew what was happening in England.

CALDICOTT: Mustn't lose grip, Charters.

A knock is heard at the door.

CALDICOTT: Come in.

ANNA *enters.*

ANNA: Pereskai (Begging your pardon).

In a series of reaction shots, we see ANNA *look at* CALDICOTT *and* CHARTERS. *She joins them.*

ANNA: Pas que roben depouli (Can I change my clothes)?

CALDICOTT: Did you follow that?

CHARTERS: I did. Tell her this has gone far enough.

CALDICOTT: No, er . . . no change . . . er here. Mm, outside.

ANNA: Pereskai (Begging your pardon).

CALDICOTT: She doesn't understand.

CHARTERS: No, come on.

CHARTERS and CALDICOTT *leave* ANNA *in her room, and walk out of the camera shot down the hotel landing. We cut to* CHARTERS *and* CALDICOTT *now in the hotel foyer. They walk to a table and pick up some newspapers.*

CHARTERS: Nothing newer than last month.

CALDICOTT: I don't suppose there is such a thing as a wireless set hereabouts.

CHARTERS: Awful being in the dark like this, you know, Caldicott.

CALDICOTT: Our communications cut off in a time of crisis.

13

The camera moves from them to BORIS *who is talking into the telephone receiver on the reception desk.*

BORIS: Hallo, hallo, hallo, London?

We see CHARTERS *and* CALDICOTT *look at one another as they overhear* BORIS'S *conversation.*

BORIS: (*into phone*) You want Mr. Seltzer? Yes, hold on. I'm going right to find him . . . where he is.

CALDICOTT *and* CHARTERS *watch* BORIS *leave, look at one another and move to the reception desk.*

CHARTERS: London!

CALDICOTT: Go on, risk it.

CHARTERS: (*into phone*) Hallo . . . hallo. You . . . you in London. What? No, no, no, I'm not Mr. Seltzer. Name's Charters. I don't suppose you know me. What? You needn't worry, they've just gone to fetch him. Tell me, what's happening to England? Blowing a gale? No, you don't follow me, sir. I'm enquiring about the Test Match in Manchester. Cricket, sir, cricket! What, you don't know? You can't be in England and not know the test score. The fellow says he doesn't know.

CALDICOTT: Silly ass.

CHARTERS: (*into phone*) Hallo, can't you find out? Oh, nonsense, it won't take a second. All right, if you won't, you won't.

CHARTERS *replaces the telephone receiver on the hook.*

CHARTERS: Wasting my time. The fellow's an ignoramus.

BORIS *enters in the background with* MR. SELTZER.

BORIS: Mr. Seltzer, at last your call's come through to London.

CHARTERS *and* CALDICOTT *look sheepishly at one another and walk away.*

BORIS *off:* (*into phone*) Hallo, hallo, hallo, karistica

14

crastica fatistica London? Me di castia London. Oh! saeme dein a-calle porte (What has happened to my call to London? I've been cut off from London . . . Oh! what clumsiness).

Cut to the interior of the dining room as CALDICOTT *and* CHARTERS *enter.* MISS FROY *is seen sitting at a table. The room is crowded. The people seated with* MISS FROY *get up to leave and* CALDICOTT, CHARTERS *and other guests are seen trying to obtain these seats.* CALDICOTT *and* CHARTERS *succeed by pushing and forcing themselves in front of the others. A* WAITER *enters.*

WAITER: Pairdum . . . (Excuse me)! Rayni cartodo escht finido . . . (There is no food left).

CHARTERS: Thank you, waiter.

WAITER: Rayni cartodo escht finido . . . (There is no food left).

CHARTERS: Well, what do you say to a grilled steak?

CALDICOTT: A very good idea. Well done for me, please.

CHARTERS: On the red side for me.

WAITER: Rayni cartodo escht finido . . . (There is no food left).

CHARTERS: These people have a passion for repeating themselves.

MISS FROY: I . . . I beg your pardon.

CHARTERS: Mm?

MISS FROY: He's trying to explain to you that owing to the large number of visitors there's no food left.

CHARTERS: No food? What sort of place is this? Do they expect us to share a blasted dog box with a servant girl on an empty stomach? Is that hospitality? Is that organisation?

The camera cuts from CHARTERS *to* CALDICOTT *to the*

WAITER *to* MISS FROY. CHARTERS'S *face registers unease as he realises he has forgotten his manners. He turns to* MISS FROY.

CHARTERS: Oh, thank you.

CALDICOTT: I'm hungry, you know.

CHARTERS: What a country! I don't wonder they have revolutions.

MISS FROY: You're very welcome to what's left of the cheese. Of course, it's not like beefsteak but it's awfully rich in vitamins.

CHARTERS: Oh, really . . . thank you very much.

MISS FROY: I'm afraid they're not accustomed to catering for so many people. Bandrika is one of Europe's few undiscovered corners.

CHARTERS: That's probably because there's nothing worth discovering, I should think.

MISS FROY: You may not know it as well as I do. I'm feeling quite miserable at the thought of leaving it.

CALDICOTT: After you with the cheese, please!

CHARTERS: Certainly, old man. Why not? You're going home.

MISS FROY: Tomorrow. My little charges are quite grown up. I'm a governess and . . . and music teacher, you know. In the six years I've lived here, I've grown to love the country. Especially the mountains. I sometimes think they're like very friendly neighbours. You know, the big father and mother mountains with their white snow hats, and their nephews and nieces, not quite so big with smaller hats.

A SINGER *can be heard playing a guitar.* CALDICOTT *and* CHARTERS *look at one another, bored with the old lady.*

MISS FROY: Right down to the tiniest hillock without any hat at all. Of course, that's just my fancy.

16

CHARTERS: Oh, really?

MISS FROY: I like to watch them from my bedroom every night when there's a moon. I'm so glad there's a moon tonight. Do you hear that music? Everyone sings here. The people are just like happy children, with laughter on their lips and music in their hearts.

CHARTERS: It's not reflected in their politics, you know.

MISS FROY: I never think you should judge any country by its politics. After all, we English are quite honest by nature, aren't we? You'll excuse me if I run away? Good night, good night.

> MISS FROY *exits.*

CHARTERS: Queer sort of bird.

CALDICOTT: Trifle whimsical, I thought.

CHARTERS: After six years in this hole we'd be whimsical.

CALDICOTT: Oh, I don't think so, old man. She was very decent about that cheese.

CHARTERS: I see she's finished the pickles.

> *Cut to the hotel corridor outside* IRIS'S *room. We see* BLANCHE, JULIE *and* IRIS *standing together.*

BLANCHE: Good night, Iris. Listen, someone's serenading.

IRIS: Oh, let him. Nothing will keep me awake tonight. Good night, my children.

> IRIS *kisses* BLANCHE *and* JULIE.
> *As the women part, we see a long shot of* IRIS *with* MISS FROY *in the foreground unlocking her bedroom door, which is next to* IRIS'S *room. We go with* MISS FROY *into her bedroom. The* SINGER *can still be heard.* MISS FROY *sways with the music. We see a quick shot of the* SINGER *and then come back to* MISS FROY *by her bedroom window, listening to the* SINGER. *Stamping and the sound of a clarinet being played can be heard from upstairs.*

MISS FROY *looks annoyed.*
In the hotel corridor we see MISS FROY *and* IRIS *coming from their rooms as the clarinet "noise" persists.*

IRIS: What's happening? An earthquake?

MISS FROY: That would hardly account for the music, would it? What a horrible noise. What can they be doing?

IRIS: I don't know, but I'll soon find out.

> *We follow* IRIS *back into her bedroom.* MISS FROY *stands in the doorway.* IRIS *sits on the side of her bed and talks into the telephone.*

IRIS: Hallo.

> *We see a shot of the chandelier vibrating.* IRIS *looks at* MISS FROY.

IRIS: Musical country this.

MISS FROY: Yes, I . . . I feel quite sorry for that poor singer outside having to compete with this.

IRIS: *(into phone)* Boris? Miss Henderson speaking. Look, someone upstairs is playing musical chairs with an elephant. Move one of them out, will you? I want to get some sleep. All right. *(putting down the telephone)* That ought to settle it.

MISS FROY: Thank you so much.

> IRIS *walks back into the corridor with* MISS FROY.

MISS FROY: Some people have so little consideration for others, which makes life so much more difficult than it need be, don't you think? Good night and thank you so much. I expect you'll be going back on the train in the morning.

IRIS: Yes.

MISS FROY: Then I hope we shall meet again under . . . under quieter circumstances. Good night.

IRIS: Good night.

MISS FROY: And thank you so much.

MISS FROY *exits and* BORIS *enters.*

BORIS: Sagri morrida . . . pierci ectenda (Miss, please, I'll fix everything).

IRIS: You'd better.

Back in IRIS'S *bedroom she sits on her bed and sighs as the chandelier continues to vibrate.*
BORIS *is seen walking along the landing above* IRIS'S *room. He stands outside* GILBERT'S *room and knocks. There is no answer.* BORIS *enters. The camera pans to include three* SERVANTS, *folk dancing to* GILBERT'S *music.* GILBERT *is sprawled across his bed, music sheets in front of him, playing his clarinet.*

GILBERT: Hold it. Splendid, don't move, don't move.

GILBERT *makes notes of the* SERVANTS' *positions on his paper, taking no notice of* BORIS.

BORIS: Er . . . If you please, sir.

GILBERT: Get out! One, two.

GILBERT *goes back to his music and the* SERVANTS *continue to dance.*

BORIS: Please, sir, will you kindly stop? They are all complaining . . . in the whole hotel. You make too much noise.

GILBERT: Too much what?

BORIS: Too much noise.

GILBERT: You dare to call it a noise. The ancient music with which your present ancestors celebrated every wedding for countless generations. The dance they danced when your father married your mother, always supposing you were born in wedlock, which I doubt. Look at them.

We see a shot of the three SERVANTS, *now motionless, trying to hold their positions as* GILBERT *is not playing*

19

his clarinet. BORIS *looks incredulous.*

GILBERT: I take it you're the manager of this hotel?

BORIS: Sure I am the manager of the hotel.

GILBERT: Fortunately I am accustomed to squalor. Tell me, who's complaining?

BORIS: The young English lady underneath.

GILBERT: Well, you tell the young English lady underneath that I am putting on record for the benefit of mankind, one of the lost folk dances of Central Europe and furthermore that she does not own this hotel. Get out!

BORIS: But, sir, you don't understand.

BORIS *exits.*

GILBERT: Now, one, two!

GILBERT *continues his studies. Meanwhile,* IRIS'S *chandelier continues to vibrate. We cut to* BORIS *now back in* IRIS'S *room.*

BORIS: And do you know what he said? "Who does she think she is, the Queen of Sheba? She thinks she owns this hotel?"

IRIS: Well, can't you get rid of him?

BORIS: Impossible.

IRIS: Are you sure?

IRIS *takes bank notes from her handbag.*

BORIS: I begin to wonder. It's come back to me. I have got an idea. You see, the German lady she will call him up on the telephone and she say "Young man, it is my room. I did pay for it. Get out quickly." How's that?

IRIS: Good enough.

BORIS: We will inject him with a little . . . he'll never forget as long as he live.

20

We are in ANNA'S *room. There is a shot of an open newspaper being held in front of the camera.*

CALDICOTT *off:* Nothing but baseball. You know, we used to call it rounders. Children play it with a rubber ball and a stick. Not a word about cricket. Americans have got no sense of proportion.

A knock is heard at the door.

CALDICOTT *calling off:* Come in.

The newspaper is moved to reveal CHARTERS *and* CALDICOTT *in bed.* ANNA *enters and looks around. Everybody looks at each other, then she turns around and leaves.* CALDICOTT *and* CHARTERS *say nothing. They are looking at each other.* ANNA *comes in again.*

ANNA: Goodernaght (Good evening).

ANNA *goes out.*

CHARTERS: Can't stand this ridiculous lack of privacy . . . lock the door.

CHARTERS *gets out of bed and we follow him to the door – in his pyjama top only. Just as he gets to the door,* ANNA *pops her head round it.*

CHARTERS: Oh!

ANNA: Goodernaght (Good evening).

The film cuts to IRIS *in bed. Without knocking,* GILBERT *enters. He leans on the doorpost in an outdoor coat and hat, with his suitcase and bags. They look at each other, camera cutting rapidly between their expressions.*

IRIS: Who are you? What do you want?

GILBERT *produces his clarinet and plays a few notes.*

GILBERT: Recognise the signature tune?

IRIS: Will you please get out?

GILBERT *enters the room and looks around. He walks towards the bed.*

GILBERT: Oh, this is a much better room. In fact, definitely an acceptable room.

There are more exchanges of glances between IRIS *and* GILBERT. GILBERT *removes her lingerie that is hanging on the bedhead, and places his hat and coat on them instead.*

IRIS *off:* What exactly do you think you're doing? Keep away!

GILBERT: Would you hold those for a minute?

GILBERT hands his clarinet to IRIS *and takes his pyjamas from a suitcase.*

IRIS: Put those back at once.

GILBERT: Now, which side do you like to sleep?

IRIS: Do you want me to throw you out?

GILBERT: Well, in that case, I'll sleep in the middle. Smart of you to bribe the manager.

GILBERT enters the bathroom and prepares to wash. IRIS *gets out of bed and follows him to the bathroom door.*

GILBERT: An eye for an eye and a tooth for a toothbrush.

IRIS: I suppose you realise you're behaving like a complete cad?

GILBERT: On the contrary, you're perfectly at liberty to sleep in the corridor if you want to.

IRIS turns and goes back to the bed. She picks up the telephone and talks into it.

IRIS: Hallo.

GILBERT: Oh, I shouldn't if I were you. I'd only tell everyone you invited me here.

There is a medium shot of IRIS *replacing the telephone receiver.*

GILBERT: And when I say everyone, I mean everyone. I have a powerful voice.

GILBERT *closes the bathroom door.*

IRIS: Come out of there at once!

GILBERT: Not until you bribe the manager to restore me to my attic.

IRIS: Come out of that bathroom.

IRIS (*into phone*): Hallo, Boris? Look, I was thinking, I might change my mind about that room upstairs . . .

We cut to GILBERT *coming from the bathroom.*

GILBERT: Oh, by the way, you might have my things taken upstairs, would you?

IRIS: You're the most contemptible person I've ever met in all my life!

GILBERT *goes to the door. He turns around as he opens it and smiles towards* IRIS.

GILBERT: Confidentially, I think you're a bit of a stinker, too.

MISS FROY leans out of her bedroom balcony, listening to the SINGER *playing the guitar.*
The SINGER *is seen performing as two hands come in to the picture and close around his throat.*
MISS FROY tosses down a coin just as the music ceases, and she moves from the window to prepare for bed.
We cut to an exterior shot of Zolney Station with a train at the platform. CALDICOTT *and* CHARTERS *are seen walking along the platform.*

CALDICOTT: If we get to Basle in time, we should see the last day of the match.

CHARTERS: Hope the weather's like this in Manchester. A perfect wicket for our fellows.

We cut to a shot of local people on the platform, together with MR. *and* MRS. TODHUNTER, *walking beside the train looking into the compartments.*

MRS. TODHUNTER: Isn't it somewhere along here?

TODHUNTER: If you don't hurry, Margaret, we shan't get that compartment to ourselves, you know.

MRS. TODHUNTER: Does it matter?

We cut to another section of the train. IRIS, JULIE *and* BLANCHE *are standing together on the platform.*

JULIE: Well, there's still time to change your mind, Iris.

BLANCHE: Yes, why not send Charles a greeting telegram and tell him he's all washed up?

IRIS: No, it's too late. This time next week, I shall be a slightly sunburnt offering on an altar in Hanover Square. I shan't mind, really.

MISS FROY *comes into the shot, walking towards the women and looking absentmindedly about her.*

MISS FROY: Ah, good morning. I can't find my bag. It's a brown hold-all, you know. Have you seen it? No, of course not. Thank you.

IRIS, JULIE *and* BLANCHE *look at each other as* MISS FROY *walks off.*

MISS FROY *off:* I gave it to the porter. I can't imagine what I could have done with it.

IRIS: Oh, she's dropped her glasses.

IRIS *bends down and picks them up from the platform and follows after* MISS FROY.
We see a window box being tipped over a ledge above MISS FROY, *as* IRIS *walks over to her.*

IRIS: You dropped your glasses.

The window box falls into the picture and hits IRIS *on the head.*

24

MISS FROY: Oh, thank you, my dear. Oh, dear, oh, dear, oh, dear!

BLANCHE *and* JULIE *enter the scene and hold* IRIS, *who is rubbing her head.*

BLANCHE: Are you hurt?

IRIS: I don't know. What was it?

GUARD: Magrabtund masca nunzo dar treni (Take your place on the train, please).

BLANCHE: Never mind about that. This cockeyed station of yours has practically brained my friend.

MISS FROY: Yes, indeed.

BLANCHE: Well, what are you going to do about it?

GUARD: Tempar mag rabtung . . . (I can't keep the train any longer).

MISS FROY: He says he can't hold the train.

JULIE: Well, I like that!

BLANCHE: Hurry up. It's going.

IRIS: I'll be all right, really.

JULIE: Are you sure?

IRIS: Yes, sure.

MISS FROY: Don't worry, I'll look after her. Such carelessness.

Men shovelling snow from the railway track are shown, as the train creaks and begins to pull very slowly away from the station.
We cut to an interior shot of a first class compartment where IRIS *is seen looking out of the window at* BLANCHE *and* JULIE *on the platform.*

BLANCHE: Are you sure you're all right?

JULIE: Send us a copy of the *Times*.

BLANCHE: Write and tell us all about it. Good luck. Look after yourself.

As the train picks up speed, we see rapid cuts to the faces of BLANCHE, JULIE *and* IRIS.
This sequence dissolves to a montage of train wheels, BLANCHE *and* JULIE.
Now dissolve back to IRIS'S *first class compartment.*

MISS FROY: There, there, you'll be all right in a minute. Just take everything quietly. Put some of this *eau de cologne* on your head.

As IRIS *pats her forehead she gazes at the other members of the compartment:* SIGNOR DOPPO, *a* CHILD, *the* BARONESS, SIGNORA DOPPO, *and back to* MISS FROY.

MISS FROY: Do you feel any better?

IRIS: Yes, thank you. I'm all right now.

MISS FROY: What you need is a good strong cup of tea. I'll ring for the attendant.

IRIS: No, no, please, don't bother. I'll go to the dining car myself. I need some air.

MISS FROY: Well, in that case, I'll come with you. If you don't mind, that is?

IRIS: No, of course not.

They walk into the corridor. As they begin carefully walking along it, MISS FROY *stumbles and falls into the* TODHUNTERS' *compartment.*

MISS FROY: Oh, I beg your pardon. I'm so sorry.

TODHUNTER *stands and closes the door and pulls down the blind.* MISS FROY *smiles at* IRIS.

MISS FROY: You can always tell a honeymoon couple, you know. They're so shy.

The scene cuts to the interior of the TODHUNTERS' *compartment. Only* MR. *and* MRS. TODHUNTER *are there.*

MRS. TODHUNTER: Why did you do that?

TODHUNTER: We don't want people staring at us.

MRS. TODHUNTER: Anyone would think the whole legal profession were dogging you.

TODHUNTER: Well, one would be enough.

MRS. TODHUNTER: You even thought that beggar in Damascus was a barrister in disguise.

TODHUNTER: I merely said his face was distinguished enough for a judge.

MRS. TODHUNTER: You hurried off in the opposite direction I noticed.

TODHUNTER: That's not true. I was looking for the street called 'Straight'.

MRS. TODHUNTER: You weren't so careful the first few days.

TODHUNTER: I know. I know.

MRS. TODHUNTER: And anyway, as for you meeting someone you know, what about me? Robert thinks I'm cruising with Mother.

We cut to an interior shot of the dining car as IRIS *and* MISS FROY *enter in the background.*

MISS FROY: If one is feeling a little bit shaky I always think it's best to sit in the middle of the coach . . . preferably facing the engine.

IRIS *and* MISS FROY *sit opposite each other. The* STEWARD *enters.* CHARTERS *and* CALDICOTT *have the table at the side of them, separated by the way through the carriage.*

MISS FROY: A pot of tea for two, please.

STEWARD: Very good, madam.

MISS FROY: Oh, and just a minute, will you please tell

27

them to make it from this. I don't drink any other. And make absolutely sure that the water is really boiling, do you understand?

We see MISS FROY *taking a package from her handbag, handing it to the* STEWARD *who leaves.*

MISS FROY: It's a little fad of mine. My dear father and mother, who I'm thankful to say are still alive and enjoying good health, invariably drink it, and so I follow their footsteps. Do you know, a million Mexicans drink it? At least that's what it says on the packet.

IRIS: It's very kind of you to help me like this. I don't think we've introduced ourselves. My name's Iris Henderson, I'm going home to be married.

MISS FROY: Really? Oh, how very exciting. I do hope you'll be happy.

IRIS: Thank you.

MISS FROY: You'll have children, won't you? They make such a difference. I always think it's being with kiddies so much that's made me, if I may say so, young for my age. I'm a governess, you know. My name's Froy.

The train has picked up speed and there is a lot of noise. IRIS *has difficulty in hearing* MISS FROY.

IRIS: Did you say Freud?

MISS FROY: No, O.Y., not E.U.D. . . Froy.

IRIS: I'm sorry I can't hear.

We see MISS FROY *solve their problem by writing her name on the window.*

MISS FROY: Froy, it rhymes with joy.

The STEWARD *enters with the tea tray.*

MISS FROY: Thank you. Please reserve two places for lunch, will you?

The STEWARD *exits.*

MISS FROY: That is, if you'd care to have it with me.

IRIS: Of course.

We move to CHARTERS *and* CALDICOTT *at the adjoining table, in deep conversation.*

CHARTERS: Nothing more about it, it simply wasn't out, that's all. But for the Umpire's blunder he'd probably still be batting.

CALDICOTT: What do you mean? I don't understand.

CHARTERS: I'll show you. Look here. I saw the whole thing.

CHARTERS *tips the sugar lumps onto the table.*

CHARTERS: Now then. There's Hammond, there's the bowler, and there's the Umpire.

We cut to MISS FROY *and* IRIS *at their table.*

MISS FROY: Sugar?

IRIS: Two, please.

MISS FROY: Dear me, there is no sugar.

MISS FROY *looks around her and sees* CHARTERS *and* CALDICOTT, *still playing with the sugar lumps.*

CHARTERS: Now watch this very, very carefully, Caldicott. Gimmett was bowling.

MISS FROY: May I trouble you for the sugar, please?

CHARTERS: What?

MISS FROY: The sugar, please.

CHARTERS *and* CALDICOTT *replace the sugar lumps in the bowl in disgust, and hand it over to* MISS FROY.

MISS FROY: Thank you so much.

We see an exterior low angle shot of the train crossing a bridge, and then cut back to IRIS *and* MISS FROY *re-entering their compartment from the corridor.*

MISS FROY: If I were you I'd try and get a little sleep. It'll make you feel quite well again. There's a most intriguing acrostic in the *Needlewoman*. I'm going to try and unravel it before you wake up.

> IRIS *settles down in her seat. She gazes quickly at the same members of her compartment and at* MISS FROY *reading, before falling asleep.*
> *A montage of shots helps convey the passing of time and miles. There are shots of the engine, telegraph wires, railway lines repeated rapidly. The camera comes back into* IRIS'S *compartment where everyone is still seated – except that* MISS FROY'S *seat is empty.*

ATTENDANT *off:* Prandoor . . . billet resach (Reservations for lunch, please).

> *The* ATTENDANT *enters and goes up to each person individually in the compartment.*

ATTENDANT: Reservations for lunch, please.

SIGNOR DOPPO: Bin may (Three please).

ATTENDANT: Daf (For the first lunch)?

SIGNOR DOPPO: Bin daf (Three places for the first lunch).

ATTENDANT: Madame has booked for lunch?

IRIS: Oh, I think my friend did. She's got the tickets.

> IRIS *gets up and looks up and down the corridor, then turns back to the compartment.*

IRIS: Have you seen my friend?

SIGNOR DOPPO: Non (No).

IRIS: My friend. Where is she? La signora Inglese. The English lady, where is she?

BARONESS: There has been no English lady here.

IRIS: What?

BARONESS: There has been no English lady here.

IRIS: But there has. She sat there in the corner.

They all look at one another. IRIS *is dumbfounded and talks directly to* SIGNOR DOPPO.

IRIS: You saw her, you spoke to her, she sat next to you. But this is ridiculous. She took me to the dining car and came back here with me.

BARONESS: You went and came back alone.

IRIS: Maybe you don't understand. I mean the lady who looked after me when I was knocked out.

SIGNOR DOPPO: Ah perhaps it make you forget, eh?

IRIS: Well I may be very dense, but if this is some sort of a joke I'm afraid I don't see the point.

IRIS *leaves the compartment. The camera follows her along the corridor and into the dining car. The* STEWARD *enters in the foreground and* IRIS *follows him out to the next corridor.*

IRIS: Oh, Steward. You served me tea just now.

STEWARD: Yes, madame.

IRIS: Have you seen the lady I was with. The English lady.

STEWARD: But madame was alone.

HEAD STEWARD *off:* Caproki Eugene (They heard Eugene).

The HEAD STEWARD *enters.*

HEAD STEWARD: Pardon, madame. He make mistake.

IRIS: Well, of course, he must remember the little English lady. She ordered the tea and paid for it.

STEWARD: No, it was you who paid.

HEAD STEWARD: Caproki (She heard).

STEWARD: Nagra additan (Look at the bill).

HEAD STEWARD: He say to look at the bill. I will look, madame.

IRIS: But she gave you a special packet of tea. You can't have forgotten that.

STEWARD: The tea was ours, madame. I received no packet.

IRIS: But you did. I know what happened.

HEAD STEWARD: Pardon, madame. The bill. Tea for one.

IRIS: But that's not right.

HEAD STEWARD: Perhaps madame would care to examine the bills herself.

IRIS: No, I wouldn't. The whole thing's too absurd.

> IRIS *leaves her compartment as the train continues its journey. She walks along the corridor and down the train until she enters a fourth class compartment.* GILBERT *is there, but she does not notice him at first.*

IRIS: Please have you seen a lady pass through . . . Oh!

GILBERT: Well, well. If it isn't Old Stinker. If I thought you were going to be on this train I'd have stayed another week in the hotel. Lady? No, why?

IRIS: It doesn't matter. You probably wouldn't recognise one anyway.

> IRIS *sways as if she is about to faint.* GILBERT *goes across to her past an old man smoking a pipe.*

GILBERT: Hallo! Feeling queer? It's that pipe of yours, George. Why don't you throw your old socks away. Never mind, thanks for the help all the same. Now, come on, sit down and take it easy. What's the trouble?

IRIS: If you must know something fell on my head.

GILBERT: When? Infancy?

IRIS: At the station.

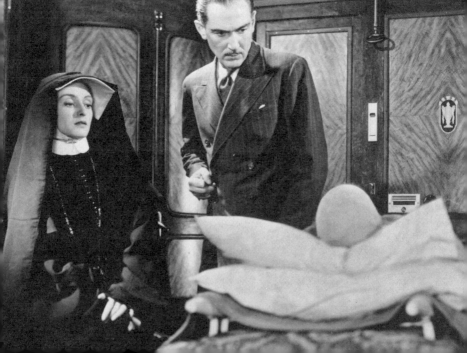

GILBERT: Oh, bad luck! Can I help?

IRIS: No, only by going away.

GILBERT: No, no, no, no, my father always taught me, never desert a lady in trouble. He even carried that as far as marrying mother.

IRIS: I say, did you see a little lady last night in the hotel in tweeds?

GILBERT: I only saw one little lady and she was hardly in tweeds.

IRIS: Yes, but she was in my compartment, and now I can't find her.

GILBERT: Well, she must be still on the train. We haven't stopped since we started.

IRIS: Of course she's still on the train. I know that.

GILBERT: All right, all right. Nobody said she isn't.

IRIS: Yes, but that's just what they are saying.

GILBERT: Who?

IRIS: The rest of the people in the compartment and the Steward. They insist they never saw her.

GILBERT: All of them?

IRIS: All of them.

GILBERT: You were saying you got a knock on the head.

IRIS: What do you mean?

GILBERT: Oh, never mind. Do you talk the lingo?

IRIS: No.

GILBERT: Oh, well, they probably thought you were trying to borrow some money. Come on, let's knock the idea out of their stupid heads. A most unfortunate remark, I beg your pardon.

IRIS *and* GILBERT *walk down the corridor, where* IRIS

41

spots SIGNOR DOPPO *and* DR. HARTZ *talking together.*

IRIS: That's one of them. The little dark man.

GILBERT: I say, excuse me. I think there's been a little misunderstanding. This young lady seems to have lost her friend.

DR. HARTZ: Yes, I have heard. The gentleman has been explaining to me. Most interesting, and I think under the circumstances we shall all introduce ourselves.

SIGNOR DOPPO: I am Italian citizen. My wife and child.

GILBERT: How do you do. Bonny little chap. How old is he?

SIGNOR DOPPO: Nineteen thirty-four class.

GILBERT: Ah!

SIGNOR DOPPO: And the lady in the corner is the Baroness Athena.

GILBERT: Oh, yes. I met her husband, and he presented prizes at the Folk Dances Festival. Minister of Propaganda.

DR. HARTZ: And I am Doctor Egon Hartz of Prague. You may have heard of me.

GILBERT: Not the brain specialist?

DR. HARTZ: The same.

GILBERT: Yes, you flew over to England the other day and operated on one of our cabinet ministers.

DR. HARTZ: Oh, yes.

GILBERT: Tell me, did you find anything?

DR. HARTZ: A slight Cerebral Confusion.

GILBERT: Oh, well, that's better than nothing.

DR. HARTZ: But I am picking up a similar case at the next station, but so much more complicated. I shall operate at the National Hospital tonight. Among other things a cranial fracture with compression. You understand?

GILBERT: Oh yes, a wallop on the bean.

IRIS: I suppose you haven't seen my friend?

DR. HARTZ: Unfortunately no.

GILBERT: I'll just take a word with the Baroness.

GILBERT *enters the first class compartment and goes towards the* BARONESS, *who is seated by the window.*

GILBERT: Bakara vaskin fermera baronak (Excuse me, have you seen an elderly lady in here, Baroness)?

BARONESS: Nagray femora (I have seen no elderly lady).

GILBERT: Excuee avete visto la Signora (Excuse me, have you seen this lady)?

SIGNORA DOPPO: Non no la seen her (No, I haven't seen her).

IRIS: What do they say?

GILBERT: Well, they both say they've never seen her.

IRIS: But that's not true. She was sitting where you are.

DR. HARTZ: Can you describe her?

IRIS: Well, it's a bit difficult. You see she was sort of middle-aged, and ordinary.

GILBERT: What was she wearing?

IRIS: Tweeds, oatmeal flecked with brown, a three-quarter coat with patch pockets, a scarf, felt hat, brown shoes, a tussore shirt and . . . and a small blue handkerchief in her breast pocket. I can't remember any more.

GILBERT: You couldn't have been paying attention. Now listen, you both went along to tea?

IRIS: Yes.

GILBERT: Well, surely you met somebody.

IRIS: I suppose we did, but wait a moment, let me think. Oh yes, there was an Englishman who passed the sugar.

GILBERT: Right you are. Now, let's go along and dig him out.

DR. HARTZ: Pardon. May I come with you? This is most interesting to me.

GILBERT: Well, we don't like people muscling in, but we'll make you a member.

IRIS: Wait a moment, there was somebody else. As we passed this compartment Miss Froy stumbled in, there was a tall gentleman and a lady.

GILBERT: Right, now we're getting somewhere. If we can really find someone who saw her, we'll have the place searched.

TODHUNTER *comes into the picture.*

TODHUNTER: Can I be of any assistance?

IRIS: That's the gentleman.

GILBERT: Well, do you happen to remember seeing this young lady pass the compartment with a little English woman?

TODHUNTER: I'm, er . . . I'm afraid not.

IRIS: But you must have. She almost fell into your compartment. Surely you haven't forgotten. It's very important. Everybody's saying she wasn't on the train, but I know she is and I'm going to find her even if I have to stop the train to do it.

CHARTERS *is in the corridor, knocking on a compartment door.*

CHARTERS: I say, Caldicott. It's Charters. Can I come in?

CALDICOTT *appears.*

CHARTERS: You know that girl we saw in the hotel? She's

44

back there kicking up a devil of a fuss, says she's lost her friend.

CALDICOTT: Well, she hasn't been in here, old man.

CHARTERS: But the point is, she threatens to stop the train.

CALDICOTT: Oh, Lord!

CHARTERS: If we miss our connection at Basle, we'll never make Manchester in time.

CALDICOTT: This is serious.

CHARTERS: Let's hide in here.

TODHUNTER: (*to* IRIS) I'm sorry, I haven't the faintest recollection. You must be making a mistake.

GILBERT: Well, he obviously doesn't remember. Let's go and look for the other fellow.

We have an interior shot of the TODHUNTERS' *compartment.*

MRS. TODHUNTER: Who were you talking to outside?

TODHUNTER: Oh, nobody . . . just some people in the corridor . . . arguing.

Back in the corridor we see GILBERT *and* IRIS *walking along as* CHARTERS *comes from the other direction.*

IRIS: There he is . . . that's the man.

GILBERT: Oh, I say, I'm so sorry – I wonder if I can bother you . . . I wonder if you can help us.

CHARTERS: How?

IRIS: Well, I was having tea about an hour ago with an English lady . . . you saw her, didn't you?

CHARTERS: Well, I don't know . . . I mean . . . I was talking to my friend, wasn't I?

CALDICOTT: Indubitably.

45

IRIS: Yes, but you were sitting at the next table . . . she turned and borrowed the sugar . . . you must remember.

CHARTERS: Oh, yes . . . I recall passing the sugar.

IRIS: Well, then you saw her.

CHARTERS: I repeat – we were deep in conversation – we were discussing cricket.

IRIS: Well, I don't see how a thing like cricket can make you forget seeing people.

CHARTERS: Oh, don't you? Well, if that's your attitude, obviously there's nothing more to be said . . . Come, Caldicott . . . thing like cricket.

   CALDICOTT *and* CHARTERS *exit*.

GILBERT: Wrong tactics . . . we should have told him we were looking for a lost cricket ball.

IRIS: Yes, but he spoke to her . . . there must be some explanation.

   DR. HARTZ enters.

DR. HARTZ: There is. Please forgive me, I'm quite possibly wrong but I have known cases where a sudden shock or blow has induced the most vivid impressions.

IRIS: I understand – you don't believe me.

DR. HARTZ: Oh, it's not a question of belief – even a simple concussion may have curious effects upon an imaginative person.

IRIS: Yes, but I can remember every little detail . . . her name . . . Miss Froy . . . everything.

DR. HARTZ: So interesting. You know, if one had time, one could trace the cause of the hallucination.

GILBERT: Hallucination?

DR. HARTZ: Oh, precisely. There is no Miss Froy. There never was a Miss Froy. Merely a vivid subjective image.

46

IRIS: But I met her last night at the hotel.

DR. HARTZ: You thought you did.

GILBERT: But what about the name?

DR. HARTZ: Oh, some past association. An advertisement or a character in a novel, subconsciously remembered. No, there is no reason to be frightened, if you are quiet and relaxed.

IRIS: Thank you very much.

DR. HARTZ *looks out of a train window.*

DR. HARTZ: Dravaka. If you will excuse me, this is where my patient comes aboard. Excuse me. Most interesting.

DR. HARTZ *exits.*

GILBERT: We're stopping.

IRIS: This is our first stop, isn't it? Well, then, Miss Froy must still be on the train. Look, you look out of this window and see if she gets off this side. I'll take the other.

GILBERT: Most interesting . . .

We see IRIS *opening the window as* GILBERT *crosses the compartment to open the window opposite* IRIS.

GILBERT: What was she dressed in? Scotch tweeds, wasn't it?

IRIS: Oatmeal tweeds.

GILBERT: I knew it had something to do with porridge.

We see an exterior shot of the station. Two ATTENDANTS *enter in the background, wheeling a* PATIENT *on a stretcher, accompanied by* DR. HARTZ *and a* NUN.

DR. HARTZ: Escht tranquir (Don't let your patient be disturbed).

NUN: Din, Doktor (Very good, Doctor).

DR. HARTZ: Gentil . . . gentil . . . Coren cara (Gently . . .

gently . . . carry her carefully).

There is a shot of GILBERT *at his window in the corridor, looking up and down the track outside.* IRIS *is seen doing the same from her compartment window. The railway lines reveal no* MISS FROY.

We cut to TODHUNTER *who is looking out of his compartment.* MRS. TODHUNTER *is in the background.*

MRS. TODHUNTER: How long does it take to get a divorce? Eric?

TODHUNTER: I'm sorry, I wasn't listening.

MRS. TODHUNTER: I said, how long does it take to get a divorce?

TODHUNTER: That depends. Why?

MRS. TODHUNTER: I was only wondering whether we could take our honeymoon next spring. I mean the official one.

TODHUNTER: The difficulties are considerable. For one thing the courts are very crowded just now. Although, I suppose we barristers ought not to complain about that. As a matter of fact with the . . . with conditions as they are now, my chances of becoming a judge are very rosy. That is if, er . . . nothing untoward occurs.

MRS. TODHUNTER: Such as you being mixed up in a divorce case yourself?

TODHUNTER: Er . . . yes.

MRS. TODHUNTER: In that first careless rapture of yours, you said you didn't care what happened.

TODHUNTER: You must think of it from my point of view. The law, like Caesar's wife, must be above suspicion.

MRS. TODHUNTER: Even when the law spends six weeks with Caesar's wife?

TODHUNTER: Look here.

48

MRS. TODHUNTER: Now, I know why you've been running around like a scared rabbit. Why you lied so elaborately a few minutes ago.

TODHUNTER: I lied?

MRS. TODHUNTER: Yes, to those people in the corridor. I heard every word you said.

TODHUNTER: It was merely that I didn't wish to be mixed up in any enquiry.

MRS. TODHUNTER: Enquiry? Just because a little woman can't be found?

TODHUNTER: That girl was making a fuss. If the woman had disappeared and I'd admitted having seen her, we might become vital witnesses. My name might even appear in the papers, coupled with yours. A scandal like that might lead anywhere . . . anywhere . . .

MRS. TODHUNTER: Yes, I suppose it might.

We cut to an exterior shot of the engine as it starts to move. Back in the carriage we focus on IRIS *and* GILBERT.

GILBERT: Nobody?

IRIS: Nobody.

GILBERT: The only things that came out my side were two bits of orange peel and a paper bag.

IRIS: I know there's a Miss Froy. She's as real as you are.

GILBERT: That's what you say and you believe it. But there doesn't appear to be anybody else who has seen her.

MRS. TODHUNTER *off:* I saw her . . .

She approaches IRIS *and* GILBERT *and joins them.*

MRS. TODHUNTER: . . . I think.

IRIS: You did?

MRS. TODHUNTER: A little woman in tweeds.

IRIS: Yes.

MRS. TODHUNTER: Wearing a three-quarter coat.

IRIS: With a scarf.

MRS. TODHUNTER: That's right. I saw her with you when you passed the compartment.

IRIS: I knew I was right. But your husband said he hadn't seen her.

MRS. TODHUNTER: Oh, he didn't notice, but as soon as he mentioned it I remembered at once.

GILBERT: You win. You know, this calls for action. Are you prepared to make a statement?

MRS. TODHUNTER: Of course, if it helps.

> DR. HARTZ *enters*.

DR. HARTZ: Ah, pardon, my patient has just arrived. The most fascinating complication.

IRIS: We have some news for you. This lady actually saw Miss Froy.

DR. HARTZ: So.

GILBERT: We are going to have the train searched.

IRIS: You'll have to think of a fresh theory now, Doctor.

DR. HARTZ: It is not necessary. My theory was a perfectly good one, the facts were misleading. I hope you will find your friend. Excuse me.

MRS. TODHUNTER: I'll be in here if you want me.

GILBERT: Right you are. Come along.

> *We cut to an interior shot of the* TODHUNTERS' *compartment as* MRS. TODHUNTER *re-enters*.

MRS. TODHUNTER: Eric, I was only going to mention that I told that girl I'd seen her friend.

TODHUNTER: What's that? Have you taken leave of your senses?

MRS. TODHUNTER: On the contrary, I've come to them.

TODHUNTER: What do you mean?

MRS. TODHUNTER: If there's a scandal, there'll be a divorce. You couldn't let me down, could you? You'd have to do the decent thing as reluctantly as only you know how.

TODHUNTER: You forget one very important thing, Margaret. Your husband would divorce you, I've no doubt, but whatever happens, my wife will never divorce me.

The camera cuts back to the corridor, where GILBERT, IRIS, *the* GUARD *and* SIGNOR DOPPO *are talking together.*

GILBERT: Well, it may seem crazy to you, but I tell you you're going to search the train.

SIGNOR DOPPO: Ah, Signorina, down there they look for you. Your friend, she come back.

IRIS: Come back?

SIGNOR DOPPO: Si, si (Yes).

IRIS: But what happened?

SIGNOR DOPPO: Oh, you go see. She tell you. Sousi (Excuse me).

GILBERT: All right, Athleston, relax. The crisis is over. Come on, let's join the lady.

Camera pans with them into the first class compartment. GILBERT *goes up to* MADAME KUMMER, IRIS *follows.*

GILBERT: Here we are.

IRIS: Miss Froy? That isn't Miss Froy.

GILBERT: Isn't it?

IRIS: No.

GILBERT: I say, it's a silly thing to say, but are you Miss Froy?

MADAME KUMMER: No, I am Madame Kummer . . . Ga dossen joelator or hockatch bat kever fronche am nond (I helped her into the carriage when she was hit on the head . . . then went to see some friends).

GILBERT: She says she helped you into the carriage after you got the biff on the head and then went to see some friends.

BARONESS: Norsk revalt de denalt rinda anglisch fomana (When she said English lady I didn't think of Madame Kummer).

GILBERT: The Baroness says as you spoke about an English lady she didn't connect her with Madame Kummer.

DR. HARTZ *comes into the picture and listens intently.*

IRIS: But she wasn't the lady I saw. It was Miss Froy.

GILBERT: Oatmeal tweeds, blouse, blue silk handkerchief.

IRIS: Yes, I know everything's the same, but it isn't her.

DR. HARTZ: I beg your pardon, when did you say you first met this Miss Froy?

IRIS: Last night at the hotel.

DR. HARTZ: Was she wearing a costume like this?

IRIS: Yes, I think she was.

DR. HARTZ: Then I must apologise. You did meet her after all.

IRIS: Then . . .

DR. HARTZ: But not on this train. In your subconscious mind you substituted for the face of **Madame Kummer** that of **Miss Froy.**

IRIS: But I didn't. I couldn't have. I tell you. I talked to her here.

GILBERT: That's very easily settled, there's an English woman on the train who said she saw her. If this lady wouldn't mind . . . Madame, abner bresen dak master cav selham (Would you mind coming with us)?

MADAME KUMMER *nods.*

MADAME KUMMER: Non . . . trar taska (No . . . not at all).

GILBERT *(in French):* Bon. Après vous, mesdames (Good. After you, ladies). What a gift of languages the fellow's got!

DR. HARTZ, GILBERT, IRIS *and* MADAME KUMMER *leave the compartment and walk along the corridor to the* TODHUNTERS' *compartment.* GILBERT *knocks.*
We cut to an interior shot of TODHUNTERS' *compartment.* TODHUNTER *opens to the door to reveal* GILBERT *first, and then* IRIS *and* MADAME KUMMER *in the background.*

GILBERT: I'm so sorry, but would you tell us please, is this the woman you saw?

IRIS: It isn't a bit like her, is it?

MRS. TODHUNTER: Yes, she's the woman.

IRIS: But it isn't, I tell you, it isn't.

GILBERT: Are you sure?

MRS. TODHUNTER: Perfectly.

IRIS: She isn't. She isn't.

MADAME KUMMER: Bragarsan (Is that all)?

GILBERT: Ascar (Yes, thank you). Well, come on, then. I'm so sorry to have troubled you.

TODHUNTER *closes the door of the compartment.*

53

MRS. TODHUNTER: Well, aren't you going to say anything? You might at least gloat, if nothing else.

TODHUNTER: What am I expected to say? You only did it to save your own skin.

IRIS *and* GILBERT *are seen walking along the corridor from the* TODHUNTERS' *compartment.*

IRIS: She was lying. I saw it in her face. They're all lying, but why, why?

GILBERT: Now, why don't you sit down and take it easy?

IRIS: Do you believe that nonsense about substituting Miss Froy's face for Madame Kummer's?

GILBERT: Well, I think any change would be an improvement.

IRIS: Listen, Miss Froy was on this train. I know she was, and nothing will convince me otherwise. Must you follow me round like a pet dog?

GILBERT: Well, let's say a watch dog. It's got all the better instincts.

IRIS: Goodbye.

IRIS *moves to her compartment.*
She imagines a picture of MISS FROY *and then* SIGNORA DOPPO; *then* MISS FROY *superimposed with the* BARONESS; *then* MISS FROY'S *face with that of* SIGNOR DOPPO; *finally she thinks of* MISS FROY *and* MADAME KUMMER.
We cut back to the corridor where GILBERT *is standing, as* IRIS *appears from her compartment in the background.*

IRIS: The Doctor was right. You're all right. I never saw Miss Froy on the train. It didn't happen, I know now.

GILBERT: I'm glad you're going to take it like that. What you want to do is to forget all about it. Make your mind a complete blank. You know, watch me, you can't go wrong.

What about a spot of something to eat, eh?

IRIS: Anything.

GILBERT: That's right, come along.

We follow IRIS *and* GILBERT *along the corridor into the dining car. They sit at the very table* IRIS *and* MISS FROY *had taken earlier.*

GILBERT: Would you like a little air?

IRIS: Thanks.

GILBERT *opens the window slightly revealing* MISS FROY'S *name still written on the train window.*

GILBERT: Do you think you could eat anything?

IRIS: I could try.

GILBERT: That's the spirit. You'll feel a different girl tomorrow.

IRIS: I hope so. I don't want to meet my fiancé a nervous wreck.

GILBERT: You're what?

IRIS: I'm being married on Thursday.

GILBERT: You're quite sure you're not imagining that?

IRIS: Positive.

GILBERT: I was afraid so. Ah, food.

IRIS: I couldn't face it.

GILBERT: You know best. Do you mind if I talk with my mouth full?

IRIS: If you must.

GILBERT: Well, since you press me. I'll begin with my father. You know, it's remarkable how many great men begin with their fathers. Oh, something to drink?

IRIS: No. Oh, yes I will, a cup of tea, please.

GILBERT: One tea, and no soup for the lady. You know, my father was a very colourful character. Amongst other things, he was strongly addicted to . . . you'll never guess.

IRIS: Harriman's Herbal Tea.

GILBERT: No, double scotches.

IRIS: A million Mexicans drink it.

GILBERT: Maybe they do, but father didn't.

IRIS: Miss Froy gave the waiter a packet of it.

GILBERT: A packet of what?

IRIS: Harriman's Herbal Tea. She said it was the only sort she liked.

GILBERT: Look here, I thought we agreed that you were going to make your mind a complete blank.

IRIS: But it's so real, I'm sure it happened.

GILBERT: Did we, or did we not?

IRIS: We did. Sorry. Go on telling me about your father.

GILBERT: Well, my father was a very remarkable man . . .

IRIS: Did he play the clarinet?

GILBERT: He did. In fact he never put it down unless it became absolutely necessary. Well, naturally I couldn't help inheriting his love of music.

IRIS: Why not?

GILBERT: That was all he left me. You know, you're remarkably attractive. Has anyone ever told you?

IRIS: We were discussing you.

GILBERT: Oh yes, of course. Do you like me?

IRIS: Not much.

GILBERT: Well, after I'd, er . . . paid my father's debts, I started to travel, before they tried to cash the cheques. At the moment, I'm writing a book on folk dancing. Would you like to buy a copy?

IRIS: I'd love to. When does it see the light of day?

GILBERT: In about four years.

IRIS: That's a very long time.

GILBERT: It's a very long book. Do you know why you fascinate me? I'll tell you. You have two great qualities I used to admire in father. You haven't any manners at all, and you're always seeing things. What's the matter?

IRIS: Look!

We cut to a shot of MISS FROY'S *name on the window, as the train passes through a tunnel. Then we are back inside the dining car studying* GILBERT *and* IRIS *at their table, and* MISS FROY'S *name on the window. The train comes out of the tunnel.*

IRIS: It's gone!

GILBERT: What's gone?

IRIS: Miss Froy's name on the window. You saw it. You must have seen it. She's on the train.

GILBERT: Steady! Steady!

GILBERT *takes a glass from a* MAN *passing the table, and offers it to* IRIS.

IRIS: No. No. We've got to find her. Something's happening to her.

GILBERT: Take it easy.

IRIS: Stop the train. Listen, everybody. There's a woman on this train. Miss Froy. Some of you must have seen her. They're hiding her somewhere. I appeal to you, all of you, to stop the train.

DR. HARTZ *and* GILBERT *enter the picture.*

IRIS: Please, help me. Please make them stop the train. Do

you hear? Why don't you do something before it's too late?

DR. HARTZ: Please. Please.

IRIS: I know you think I'm crazy, but I'm not. I'm not. For heaven's sake, stop this train. Leave me alone. Leave me alone.

We follow IRIS *across the dining car, and see her pulling the communication cord. Then she faints.*
There is an interior shot of CHARTERS' *compartment.* CHARTERS *and* CALDICOTT *are sitting opposite each other.*

CHARTERS: Ten minutes late, thanks to that fool of a girl. If she gets up to any more of her tricks, we shall be too late for the last day of the match.

CALDICOTT: I suppose you couldn't put it to her in some way.

CHARTERS: What?

CALDICOTT: Well, people just don't vanish and so forth.

CHARTERS: But she has.

CALDICOTT: What?

CHARTERS: Vanished.

CALDICOTT: Who?

CHARTERS: The old dame.

CALDICOTT: Yes.

CHARTERS: Well?

CALDICOTT: But how could she?

CHARTERS: What?

CALDICOTT: Vanish.

CHARTERS: I don't know.

CALDICOTT: That just explains my point. People don't just disappear into thin air.

CHARTERS: It's done in India.

CALDICOTT: What?

CHARTERS: The rope trick.

CALDICOTT: Oh, that. It never comes out in a photograph.

The film cuts to an interior shot of the corridor. From the corridor we see DR. HARTZ *and* IRIS *in the compartment.* GILBERT *is in the corridor.*

DR. HARTZ: Look now. In half an hour we stop at Morsken, just before the border. I will leave there with my patient for the National Hospital. If you will come with me, you could stay overnight in a private ward. You need peace and rest.

IRIS: Sorry. Nothing doing.

GILBERT *off:* Isn't there anything we can do?

IRIS: Yes, find Miss Froy.

DR. HARTZ: I tell you, my friend, if she does not rest I will not answer for her. It will be best if you persuade her. She likes you.

GILBERT: I'm just about as popular as a dose of strychnine.

DR. HARTZ: If you coat it with sugar, she may swallow it.

While GILBERT *is still in the corridor, the camera pans to the* CHEF, *as he appears with a bucket of rubbish, which he throws out of the window. A piece of paper sticking to a window is seen by* GILBERT. *He notices it is part of a Harriman's Herbal Tea packet.*
GILBERT *enters the first class compartment. We see a shot of* SIGNOR DOPPO *and the* BARONESS. GILBERT *goes up to* IRIS.

GILBERT: Cosmopolitan train this. People of all nations. I've just seen at least a million Mexicans in the corridor. Well, I thought I'd look in to tell you to think over what Doctor Hartz said. If you feel like changing your mind, I'll be hanging around.

IRIS *follows* GILBERT *out into the corridor.*

IRIS: What's all the mystery?

GILBERT: You're right. Miss Froy is on this train. I've just seen the packet of tea that you are talking about. They chucked it out with the rubbish.

IRIS: You're a trifle late, aren't you? She may be dead by now.

GILBERT: Dead or alive we'll . . .

MADAME KUMMER *comes to join them.*

GILBERT: For sheer variety, give me an English summer. I remember once spending a Bank holiday at Brighton . . .

MADAME KUMMER *exits.*

GILBERT: Come on, we're going to search this train. There's something definitely queer in the air.

We cut to an exterior long shot of the train as it continues on its way, before we cut to the interior of the fourth class compartment as GILBERT *and* IRIS *pass through. They enter the luggage van.*

GILBERT: Looks like a supply service for trunk murderers.

IRIS: Don't!

There is a long shot of a wicker basket which is moving.

IRIS: What's that?

GILBERT: It's all right, Miss Froy, it's only us.

IRIS: Hurry up. Quickly.

GILBERT *opens the lid of the basket revealing a calf.*

GILBERT: Maybe it's Miss Froy bewitched. You never know. Well, anyway, I refuse to be discouraged. Faint heart never found old lady. By the way, do you know anything about her?

IRIS: No. Only that she was a governess going back home.

What is in this thing?

GILBERT: Can't imagine. Wait a minute. There might be something down here.

There is a shock as they discover a model of SIGNOR DOPPO. IRIS *and* GILBERT *look at one another.*

IRIS: What on earth!

GILBERT: Our Italian friend. I've got it. Wait a minute. There you are, the great Doppo.

GILBERT *unrolls a poster.*

GILBERT: His visiting card. Look!

IRIS: What's it say?

GILBERT: The Great Doppo. Magician, illusionist, mind reader. Signor Doppo will appear in all the principal towns and cities. See his fascinating act, The Vanishing . . . Lady.

IRIS: The Vanishing Lady?

GILBERT: Perhaps that's the explanation.

IRIS: What?

GILBERT: Maybe he was practising on Miss Froy.

IRIS: Well, perhaps it's a publicity stunt.

GILBERT: No, I don't think so. That wouldn't account for the Baroness or Madame Kummer.

IRIS: Well, what's your theory?

GILBERT: I don't know. My theory? I'll tell you.

GILBERT *accidentally unfastens a basket in the background. Pigeons fly out of it.*

IRIS: Oh, dear . . . I can't get this one.

GILBERT *goes into a trick cabinet.*

IRIS: Where are you?

We see a medium shot of the trick cabinet. GILBERT'S

voice comes from it as IRIS *stands next to it.*

GILBERT *off:* I'm in here with a strong smell of camphor balls.

IRIS: I can't see you.

GILBERT *off:* I'm about somewhere.

IRIS *enters the trick cabinet as* GILBERT *reappears.*

GILBERT: Here I am. Where are you?

IRIS *off:* I don't know.

GILBERT: That's what comes of not saying Abracadabra.

We cut to a shot of a rabbit in the trick cabinet.

IRIS *off:* Oh!

We cut to IRIS *and* GILBERT, *now both happily out of the trick cabinet and back in the luggage van together.*

IRIS: Ouch!

GILBERT: Are you hurt?

IRIS: Not much.

GILBERT: Come and sit down over here.

IRIS: What is that thing?

GILBERT: Well, in magic circles, we call it the disappearing cabinet. You get inside and vanish.

IRIS: Mm . . . so I noticed. You were about to tell me your theory.

GILBERT: Oh, my theory. Well . . .

GILBERT *puts on a Sherlock Holmes hat. His hand comes into the picture.*

GILBERT *off:* . . . My theory, my dear Watson . . .

Resume shot of GILBERT *and* IRIS.

GILBERT: . . . is that we are in very deep waters indeed.

IRIS *hands a pipe to* GILBERT.

GILBERT: Oh, thank you very much. Let us marshal our facts over a pipeful of Baker Street shag. In the first place, a little old lady disappears. Everyone that saw her promptly insists that she was never there at all. Right?

IRIS: Right.

GILBERT: We know that she was. Therefore, they did see her. Therefore, they are deliberately lying. Why?

IRIS: I don't know. I'm only Watson.

GILBERT: Well, don't bury yourself in the part. I'll tell you why. Because they daren't face an enquiry, because Miss Froy's probably still somewhere on this train.

IRIS: I told you that hours ago.

GILBERT: Oh, yes, so you did. For that, my dear Watson, you shall have a 'trichonoply" cigar.

IRIS: Oh, thank you.

GILBERT: Now, there's only one thing left to do, you know. Search the train in disguise.

IRIS: As what?

GILBERT: Well, er . . . Old English Gentleman.

IRIS: They'd see through you.

GILBERT: Perhaps you're right. Ah, Will Hay. No, boys, boys, which of you has stolen Miss Froy? Own up. Own up.

GILBERT *has perched glasses on his nose.*

IRIS: Those glasses. Give them to me.

GILBERT: Why?

IRIS: They're Miss Froy's.

GILBERT: Are you sure?

IRIS: Yes. They're exactly the same. Gold-rimmed with . . . Where did you find them?

GILBERT: Why, down here on the floor. The glass is broken.

IRIS: Well, probably in a struggle.

GILBERT: Pick up the glass, Do you realise that this is our first piece of really tangible proof?

We cut to SIGNOR DOPPO'S *hand taking* MISS FROY'S *spectacles from* IRIS'S *hand. Pan up to show* GILBERT, SIGNOR DOPPO *and* IRIS.

SIGNOR DOPPO: Will you please give me those spectacles? They belong to me. My spectacles, please.

GILBERT: Yours? Are you sure?

SIGNOR DOPPO: Dietemmi questi occhiali (You doubt my word)?

GILBERT: Ah, naughty, naughty. That's a very large nose for a very small pair of spectacles. So that's the game, is it? We'll soon see about that. These are Miss Froy's glasses and you know it. She's been in here and you know that too.

There is a shot of the calf in the wicker basket, before we cut back to GILBERT *and* SIGNOR DOPPO *struggling on the floor.*

GILBERT: Well, don't stand hopping about there like a referee, cooperate. Kick him. See if he's got a false bottom. Wait a minute, I'll get him up.

There is a quick shot of three white rabbits, then the camera focuses on IRIS *as she kicks* GILBERT.

GILBERT: Ouch! That doesn't help.

We have another shot of the white rabbits, followed by a shot of GILBERT *and* SIGNOR DOPPO *still struggling with each other.*

GILBERT: Quick, pull his ears back. Give them a twist.

GILBERT *and* SIGNOR DOPPO *continue to fight. There seems little* IRIS *can do.*

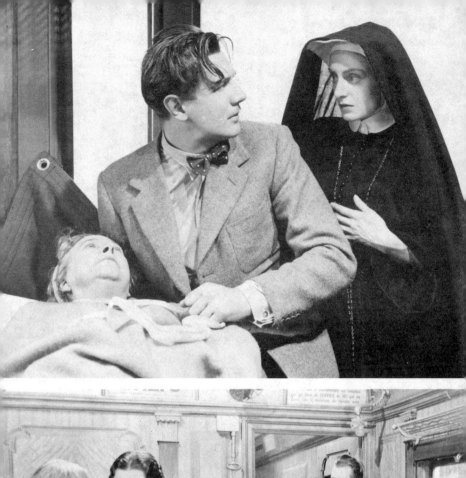

GILBERT: Look out, he's got a knife.

We cut to a close-up shot of the knife in SIGNOR DOPPO'S *hand.*

GILBERT: Try and get hold of it before he cuts a slice off me.

IRIS: I can't reach it.

The camera pans to IRIS'S *feet and legs standing on a case. As the men's fight comes closer to her, she bends down and bites* SIGNOR DOPPO'S *hand and he drops the knife.* GILBERT *comes into the picture.*

GILBERT: Well done!

There is another shot of the calf in the wicker basket, before we cut back to SIGNOR DOPPO *and* GILBERT, *who punches him on the jaw.* DOPPO *staggers back into the trick cabinet.*
Cut to DOPPO *coming out of the cabinet, with* IRIS *on the right.*

GILBERT *off:* We know how that thing works. Come out of there.

IRIS *hits* SIGNOR DOPPO *on the head.*

GILBERT: Is he out, do you think? We've got to hide him somewhere. I wonder what's in here?

IRIS: Hurry up! Quick, before he comes to.

GILBERT *lifts the lid of a nearby wooden box.*

GILBERT: It's empty. Bring him along. Oh no, you don't.

GILBERT *places* SIGNOR DOPPO *in the wooden box.*
Cut to IRIS *and* GILBERT *sitting on the box.*

GILBERT: Oh!

IRIS: What's the matter?

GILBERT: Garlic. I'll be all right in a minute. Here, hold onto this.

73

IRIS: Oh, yes.

GILBERT: Tie him up. Oh, well, we're getting somewhere at last. We definitely know that Miss Froy was on this train and we know that our friend in here had something to do with it. That ought to keep him quiet until we find her. Ah, hard work, but worth it. Let's have the evidence.

IRIS: Evidence?

GILBERT: Yes, the glasses.

IRIS: You've got them.

GILBERT: No. I haven't got them.

IRIS: Oh!

GILBERT: He's got them.

We cut to a shot of the inside of the box, which is empty.

IRIS *off:* He isn't there.

GILBERT *off:* Snookered. It's a false bottom. The twister! He's a contortionist.

Pan up to IRIS *and* GILBERT.

IRIS: He's gone all right.

GILBERT: Yes, to find the others and make more trouble. We're in a nasty jam, my dear. We can't fight the whole train. We need allies.

IRIS: Yes, but who can we trust?

GILBERT: That's the snag.

IRIS: There's that Doctor Hartz person.

GILBERT: Yes, you're right. He might help. Come on, let's tell him the symptoms.

IRIS: All right. Oh, wait a minute.

GILBERT *and* IRIS *go back through the train to find* DR. HARTZ. *They stand in the corridor outside the sleeper compartment.*

74

Only the BANDAGED PATIENT *and a* NUN *are inside, so* GILBERT *goes back into the corridor.*

GILBERT: He's not there. I've just had a particularly idiotic idea.

IRIS: Mm, I can quite believe that.

GILBERT: Suppose that patient in there is Miss Froy?

IRIS: Yes. But it didn't come on the train until after Miss Froy had disappeared.

GILBERT: Oh, yes. Yes, that's why it's an idiotic idea. Come on, let's find the doctor.

IRIS: No, no, wait a minute.

GILBERT: What is it?

IRIS: Did you notice anything wrong about that Nun?

GILBERT: No.

IRIS: I don't think she's a Nun at all. They don't wear high heels.

There is a quick flashback shot to the NUN'S *feet wearing high-heeled shoes as seen by* GILBERT

GILBERT: Yes, you're right. Listen, did you see Madame Kummer get on the train?

IRIS: No.

GILBERT: Supposing they decoyed Miss Froy into the luggage van and hid her there. At the first stop the patient comes aboard. Head injury, all wrapped up. The patient is Madame Kummer. Madame Kummer becomes Miss Froy and Miss Froy becomes that.

IRIS: Yes. But why should they go to all this trouble to kidnap a harmless little governess?

GILBERT: It isn't a governess at all. Perhaps it's some political thing, you know. Come on, let's investigate.

IRIS *and* GILBERT *enter the sleeping compartment.*

75

GILBERT: Parlez vous Français (Do you speak French)?
Sprechen sie Deutsch (Do you speak German)?
Yarka dar Bandrieken (Do you speak Bandrieken)?
Oh, well, you'll just have to put up with it in English. Can I take a look at your patient, please? Thank you. (*to* IRIS) Keep an eye on the Nun.

GILBERT *stands over the bandaged patient as* IRIS *and the* NUN *look on.* DR. HARTZ *opens the door.*

DR. HARTZ: What are you doing here? Why are you in here? This is a most serious accident case. You have no business to be here at all, neither of you.

GILBERT: Doctor Harz, we want you to undo those bandages and le us take a look at your patient's face.

DR. HARTZ: Are you out of your senses? There is no face there. Nothing but lumps of raw flesh. Already the case has lost so much blood, nothing but a transfusion can save him. What do you want me to do? Murder my patient?

GILBERT: You're quite sure that this is your patient?

IRIS: We . . . we believe it's Miss Froy.

DR. HARTZ: Miss Froy, You can't be serious. What on earth put such ideas into your heads? I understand she is deaf and dumb.

IRIS: But she may lip read.

DR. HARTZ: Oh, that's impossible. Well, in that case, perhaps you will join me in the dining car? I'll be with you in a moment. I want to be certain my patient hasn't been disturbed.

GILBERT *and* IRIS *go out of the compartment.*

DR. HARTZ: Cadeskan barogne sar calto drunk (Why did they become suspicious)?

NUN: How the devil do I know how they cottoned on? Somebody must have tipped them off. You never said the old girl was English.

76

DR. HARTZ: What difference does that make? In a few moments I shall order three drinks in the dining car. Mine will be Chartreuse. Now, one of the stewards is working for us. Now, listen carefully.

We cut to an interior shot of IRIS *and* GILBERT *entering the dining car.* CHARTERS *and* CALDICOTT *are also there.*

CHARTERS: There's that girl again.

CALDICOTT: Seems to have recovered. Lucky it blew over.

GILBERT *and* IRIS *are now seated as* DR. HARTZ *enters.*

DR. HARTZ: And now, perhaps, you'll tell me what it's all about?

GILBERT: Now, listen, Doctor, have you ever actually seen your patient?

DR. HARTZ: No, I merely received a message to pick the case up and operate at Morsken.

GILBERT: How do you know that it's not Miss Froy?

IRIS: We believe there's been a substitution, Doctor.

DR. HARTZ: You really mean to say that you think that someone has . . . (*He speaks to a* STEWARD) I want a Green Chartreuse. Won't you join me?

GILBERT: Oh, thanks. I'd like a large brandy, please.

DR. HARTZ: And you?

IRIS: I don't want anything, thanks.

GILBERT: Oh, come, it'll do you good.

IRIS: No, really, I don't want it.

DR. HARTZ: You are very tired. It will pick you up.

IRIS: All right, then. Just a small one.

DR. HARTZ: Two brandies and a Chartreuse.

GILBERT: Tell me, do you know anything about the Nun

77

who is looking after your patient?

DR. HARTZ: Nun? No. Only that she is from a convent close to where the accident occurred.

GILBERT: Don't you think it's rather peculiar that she's wearing high-heeled shoes?

DR. HARTZ: Oh, is she? Well, that is rather . . . rather curious, isn't it?

IRIS: It's a conspiracy. That's all it can be. All these people on the train say they haven't seen Miss Froy, but they have. We know that, because just now in the luggage van . . .

Her voice has risen and CHARTERS *and* CALDICOTT *notice this.*

CHARTERS: She's off again!

CALDICOTT: I hope she doesn't create another scene. Puts the lid on our getting back in time, if she did.

We cut back to a shot of the table that GILBERT, IRIS *and* DR. HARTZ *are sitting at.*

IRIS: . . . And then this fellow from the carriage, Doppo's his name, he came along and grabbed the glasses.

GILBERT: And then we went for him and had a bit of a fight.

DR. HARTZ: Oh, a fight?

IRIS *off:* We knocked him out.

DR. HARTZ: Oh!

SIGNOR DOPPO *walks past them between the tables.*

DR. HARTZ: He seems to have made a speedy recovery.

GILBERT: Yes. Oh, that's just bluff.

The STEWARD'S *hand comes in to shot with the drinks.*

STEWARD: Gratsia (Thank you).

There is a quick shot of SIGNOR DOPPO *sitting nearby,*

78

followed by another shot of the drinks on the table as DR. HARTZ'S *hand comes into the shot.*

DR. HARTZ: Oh, but how could he be involved in a conspiracy? Look at him . . . the poor fellow. He's just a harmless traveller.

GILBERT: He's also a music-hall artist making a tour of Bandrieka.

DR. HARTZ: Well?

GILBERT: And the Baroness's husband is Minister of Propaganda. One word from her and his tour would be cancelled.

DR. HARTZ: Oh, I see.

GILBERT: As for the stewards, if they don't do what they're told, they've got a nice cosy brick wall to lean up against.

Shots of the drinks on the table intersperse themselves with the conversation.

DR. HARTZ: But . . . but . . . tell me about the two English travellers over there. They also denied seeing her?

GILBERT: British diplomacy, Doctor. Never climb a fence if you can sit on it. Old Foreign Office proverb.

DR. HARTZ: What I cannot understand is why should anyone want to dispose of the old lady?

GILBERT: Well, that's just what stumps us. All we know is that she was here on this train and now she's . . .

GILBERT *swallows his drink. We see* GILBERT'S *hand replacing his glass on the table.*

GILBERT *off:* . . . gone.

DR. HARTZ: Well, if you're right, it means the whole train is against us.

IRIS: What are we going to do?

DR. HARTZ: Well, in view of what you've just told me, I

shall risk examining the patient. One moment, we mustn't act suspiciously. Behave as if nothing had happened. Drink, that'll steady your nerves. To our health. And may our enemies, if they exist, be unconscious of our purpose. Let's go. We must hurry now.

GILBERT *off:* Come on, drink up.

We see IRIS *drinking her brandy before they all go back into the corridor.*

DR. HARTZ: Wait in here.

GILBERT: Right you are.

DR. HARTZ *watches* IRIS *and* GILBERT *enter the compartment before moving on to the sleeper compartment. He enters it.*

NUN: Anything wrong?

DR. HARTZ: Nothing, except they noticed you were wearing high heels. However it makes no difference. We shall reach Morsken in three minutes. Quite an eventful journey.

GILBERT *and* IRIS *are sitting, waiting, in their compartment as* DR. HARTZ *enters.*

IRIS: Well?

DR. HARTZ: Yes, the patient is Miss Froy. She will be taken off the train at Morsken in about three minutes. She will be removed to the hospital there and operated on. Unfortunately the operation will not be successful. Oh, I should perhaps have explained, the operation will be performed by me.

GILBERT *moves towards the door.* DR. HARTZ *holds a gun in his pocket.*

DR. HARTZ: You see, I am in this conspiracy as you term it. You are a very alert young couple, but it's quite useless for you to think, as you are undoubtedly doing, of a way out of your dilemma. The drink you had just now, I regret to

80

say, contained a quantity of Hydrocin. For your benefit, Hydrocin is a very little known drug which has the effect in a small quantity of paralysing the brain and rendering the victim unconscious for a considerable period. In a slightly larger quantity, of course, it induces madness. However you have my word the dose was a normal one.

IRIS *falls over in a faint.*

DR. HARTZ: In a very few moments now you will join your young friend. Need I say how sorry I am having to take such a, how shall I say, melodramatic course. But your persistent meddling made it necessary.

GILBERT *falls back.* DR. HARTZ *leaves the compartment. As he does so,* GILBERT *opens his eyes.*

GILBERT: Are you all right? You must have fainted. Listen, there's a woman next door going to be murdered and we've got to get moving before this stuff takes effect.

IRIS: I did read once that if you keep on the go you can stay awake.

GILBERT: Right, come on, let's get going. It's locked. We can't go that way, we'll be spotted.

GILBERT *starts to open the train window.*

IRIS: You can't do that.

GILBERT: Don't worry, it's only next door, you carry on keeping fit, touch your toes, stand on your head, do anything, only whatever you do, don't fall asleep.

We have an exterior shot of GILBERT *climbing out of the window. Another train is approaching. Cut to the interior of the sleeper compartment where the* NUN *and the* PATIENT *are.*
GILBERT *appears in the background and climbs through the window of the sleeper. He and the* NUN *exchange glances.*

NUN: Go on, you needn't be afraid, it is Miss Froy. It's all right, you haven't been drugged. He told me to put

81

something in your drinks, but I didn't do it.

We see GILBERT *untying* MISS FROY'S *bandages.*

GILBERT: Who the devil are you? He said you were deaf and dumb.

NUN: Never mind about that now. If you want to save her, you've got to hurry.

The NUN *watches as* GILBERT *continues to unwrap the bandages, and* MISS FROY *is indeed revealed.*

NUN: Hartz will be back in a minute. What's going to happen then?

GILBERT: If we can hold them off until we get past Morsken, the frontier's a few miles beyond the station.

MADAME KUMMER *enters in the background.* GILBERT *claps his hand over her mouth.*

NUN: Come on, there's still time.

We move to the interior of the first class compartment, where SIGNOR DOPPO, *the* BARONESS *and* DR. HARTZ *are seated.*

DR. HARTZ: Arkda duk jova set . . . finiki (Two thousand, three thousand, four thousand, five thousand, that's the lot).

SIGNOR DOPPO: Cinque cente sememe monte dope tutto quelle che koha fatto cos poi de quest' orrechio marsicato de quelle ragazzo. (Only five thousand for all the work that I've done, it's not enough, I want some more).

BARONESS: Margordavsay (Give it to him).

We cut back to the interior of the sleeper compartment.

GILBERT: That's Morsken. Have you finished?

GILBERT *opens the door to reveal* IRIS *in the next compartment touching her toes.*

GILBERT: Come on, Miss Froy.

82

GILBERT *gives* IRIS *a slap.*

GILBERT: Come on, kid, you're not drugged. I'll explain later. Abracadabra.

MISS FROY *enters.*

IRIS: Miss Froy! Oh, I can't believe it.

MISS FROY: Thank you, my dear. Thank you very much.

GILBERT: Careful.

DR. HARTZ *enters the sleeper compartment where the* NUN *is sitting beside* MADAME KUMMER, *who is lying swathed in bandages.*

DR. HARTZ: Ready?

NUN: Yes.

DR. HARTZ *checks the other compartment and sees* GILBERT *and* IRIS *who appear to be unconscious.* MISS FROY *is secretly hidden in the toilet.*

DR. HARTZ: *(to a Guard)* Teraner lena derafo, legas cheto (Keep this door locked).

Back in the compartment, GILBERT *and* IRIS *get up. Pan round as* GILBERT *opens the door to the toilet to reveal* MISS FROY.

GILBERT: Are you all right, Miss Froy?

MISS FROY: Yes, thank you. It's rather like the rush hour on the Underground.

There is a quick, exterior long shot of the train.

GILBERT: We're slowing down!

The camera shoots through the compartment window onto a long shot of an ambulance waiting at the station. DR. HARTZ *leaves the train, and the stretcher bearing* MADAME KUMMER *is taken into a waiting ambulance.* GILBERT *and* IRIS *watch.*
Cut to the interior of the ambulance.

DR. HARTZ: Davara . . . davara (Excellent . . . excellent). I'm sorry you've had such an uncomfortable journey, Miss Froy.

DR. HARTZ unwraps the bandages and discovers his patient is MADAME KUMMER.

DR. HARTZ: Eranaverek (Damnation).

DR. HARTZ bursts from the ambulance just as the NUN is about to leave the train.

DR. HARTZ: Get back on the train.

People on the platform look at DR. HARTZ. They are puzzled.
GILBERT and IRIS are seen waiting anxiously in the compartment.

IRIS: I hope nothing goes wrong. Aren't we stopping rather a long time?

There is a long shot of the ambulance moving off as seen from the train.

GILBERT: The ambulance is going. We'll be off in a jiffy.

There is an exterior, medium-length shot of a carriage being uncoupled from the rest of the train with DR. HARTZ watching. Then we cut back to the interior of the compartment where GILBERT, IRIS and MISS FROY are.

GILBERT: Another couple of minutes, we'll be over the border.

We cut to the interior of the BARONESS'S sleeper, where the NUN, the BARONESS and DR. HARTZ are.

BARONESS: Briden dan karvik jasconey pas hafdon ragenok mantado pondalat (So this is how you repay us, those who treated you so well).

NUN: I know I've been well paid, and I've done plenty of dirty work for it, but this was murder, and she was an Englishwoman.

84

BARONESS: You are Bandriekan.

NUN: My husband was, but I'm English and you were going to butcher her in cold blood.

DR. HARTZ: Your little diversion made it necessary not only to remove the lady in question, but two others as well.

NUN: You can't do that.

DR. HARTZ: Also, it would be unwise of us to permit the existence of anyone who cannot be trusted.

NUN: You wouldn't dare. I know too much.

BARONESS: Precisely.

We cut back to the compartment where GILBERT *and* IRIS *are.*

GILBERT: I think we're over the border now. You can come out, Miss Froy.

MISS FROY *appears.*

MISS FROY: Oh, bless me. What an unpleasant journey.

GILBERT: Never mind, you shall have a corner seat for the rest of the way. There you are. Look here, now that it's over, I think you ought to tell us what's it's all about.

A scream is heard.

GILBERT: What was that scream?

IRIS: Surely it was only the train whistle.

GILBERT: It wasn't, it was a woman.

MISS FROY: Be careful.

GILBERT *enters the corridor. He reacts as he finds that the carriage has been disconnected from the rest of the train. Then he goes back into the compartment.*

GILBERT: They've rumbled. We're on a branch line and they've slipped the rear part of the train.

MISS FROY: Oh dear! Oh dear!

GILBERT: Look here! Who are you, and why are these people going to these lengths to get hold of you?

MISS FROY: I really haven't the faintest idea. I'm a children's governess. You know, I can only think they've made some terrible mistake.

GILBERT: Why are you holding out on us? Tell us the truth. You got us involved in this fantastic plot. You might at least trust us.

MISS FROY: I really don't know, I . . .

GILBERT: I wonder if there's anybody else left on the train?

IRIS: There's only the dining car in front, but there won't be anybody there now.

GILBERT: What time do you make it, tea time? All the English will be there. I'm going to have a look. Come on, we'd better stick together.

> GILBERT *is correct. Having made their way along the corridor,* MISS FROY, GILBERT *and* IRIS *enter the dining car. There are* MR. *and* MRS. TODHUNTER, CHARTERS *and* CALDICOTT.

CHARTERS: There's the old girl turned up.

CALDICOTT: Told you it was a lot of fuss about nothing. Bolt must have jammed.

GILBERT: I've got something to say. Will you all please listen? An attempt has been made to abduct this lady by force. And I've got reason to believe that the people who did it are going to try again.

CHARTERS: What the devil's the fellow drivelling about?

GILBERT: Well, if you don't believe me, you can look out of the window. This train has been diverted onto a branch line.

TODHUNTER: What are you talking about?

GILBERT: There's been . . .

TODHUNTER: Abduction . . . diverted trains . . .

IRIS: We're telling you the truth.

TODHUNTER: I'm not in the least interested. You . . . you've annoyed us enough with your ridiculous stories.

CHARTERS: My dear chap, you must have got hold of the wrong end of the stick somewhere.

CALDICOTT: Yes, things like that just don't happen.

MISS FROY: We're not in England now.

CALDICOTT: I don't see what difference that makes.

IRIS: We're stopping.

We cut to a long shot of two cars parked in a wood, as seen from the train.

GILBERT: Look, you see those cars, they're here to take Miss Froy away.

CALDICOTT: Nonsense. Look, there go a couple of people.

We cut to a long shot of DR. HARTZ *and the* BARONESS *walking towards the cars, still seen from the train.*

CALDICOTT: The cars have obviously come to pick them up.

GILBERT: Well, in that case, why go to the trouble of uncoupling the train and diverting it?

CALDICOTTT: Uncoupling?

GILBERT: There's nothing left of the train beyond the sleeping car.

CALDICOTT: There must be. Our bags are in the first class carriage.

GILBERT: Not any longer. Would you like to come and look?

CALDICOTT: If this is a practical joke, I warn you I shan't think it very funny.

GILBERT *opens the dining car door to reveal the* NUN *who is gagged.*

CALDICOTT: Good Lord!

GILBERT: Let's have some of that brandy.

They all gather around the NUN.

CHARTERS: You don't suppose there's something in this fellow's story, Caldicott, do you?

CALDICOTT: Seems a bit queer.

CHARTERS: I mean, after all, people don't go about tying up nuns.

IRIS: Someone's coming.

We cut to a long shot of an OFFICER *walking towards the train. Everyone in the dining car looks out of the window and watches the* OFFICER'S *progress.*

TODHUNTER: They can't possibly do anything to us. We're British subjects.

The OFFICER *enters the dining car. Track and pan with him to include the group.*

OFFICER: I have come to offer the most sincere apologies. An extremely serious incident has occurred . . . an attempt has been made to interfere with passengers on this train.

We see the NUN *whispering to* GILBERT.

OFFICER: Fortunately it was brought to the notice of the authorities. And so if you will be good enough to accompany me to Morsken, I will inform the British Embassy at once. Ladies and gentlemen, the cars are at your disposal.

CALDICOTT: We're very grateful. It's lucky some of you fellows understand English.

OFFICER: Well, I was at Oxford.

CHARTERS: Oh really, so was I.

GILBERT: Hold on, this woman . . . seems to be trying to say something. I don't understand the language, but it may be important. Would you . . .

OFFICER: Certainly.

The OFFICER *bends down to the* NUN *. As he does so,* GILBERT *picks up a chair and hits the* OFFICER *on the head with it. The* OFFICER *falls to the floor.*

GILBERT: That's fixed him. That's all right. He's only stunned.

The STEWARD *and* CHIEF STEWARD *look on in amazement.* GILBERT *takes the* OFFICER'S *gun.*

CALDICOTT: What the blazes did you do that for?

GILBERT: Well, I was at Cambridge.

CALDICOTT: Well, what's that got to do with it? You heard what he said, didn't you?

GILBERT: I heard what he said. That was a trick to get us off the train.

TODHUNTER: I don't believe it. The man's explanation was quite satisfactory.

CHARTERS: A thing like this might cause a war.

There is a cut to an exterior shot of the woods, where the STEWARD *is talking to the* BARONESS *and* DR. HARTZ.

STEWARD: Madra avendra . . . offichara ditata (Terrible things are happening . . . the Officer has been stunned).

Cut back to the dining car.

CHARTERS: I'm going outside to tell them what's occurred. It's up to us to apologise and put the matter right.

In the woods we see the BARONESS, DR. HARTZ, *and a* SOLDIER.

BARONESS: Brancka (Fire)!

CHARTERS *starts to climb down out of the train, but a* SOLDIER *fires from the wood.* CHARTERS *returns quickly to the dining car, shot in the hand.*

CHARTERS: You were right. Do you mind, old man?

CALDICOTT: Certainly.

CALDICOTT *wraps a handkerchief around* CHARTERS'S *hand. We see* DR. HARTZ, *the* BARONESS *and some* SOLDIERS *by the cars as seen from the train.*
DR. HARTZ *beckons the* CHIEF STEWARD.
MISS FROY, IRIS, CHARTERS, TODHUNTER *and* GILBERT *are still in the dining car.*

CHARTERS: Looks as if they mean business.

GILBERT: I'm afraid so.

TODHUNTER: They can't do anything. It would mean an international situation.

MISS FROY: It's happened before.

We see a long shot of DR. HARTZ *and* SOLDIERS *walking towards the train.*

IRIS: They're coming.

NUN: Don't let them in. They'll murder us. They daren't let us go now.

There is a long shot of DR. HARTZ *and* SOLDIERS *standing by the train.*

DR. HARTZ: I order you to surrender at once.

GILBERT: Nothing doing. If you come any nearer, I'll fire. I've warned you.

GILBERT *fires and one of the* SOLDIERS *falls.*

GILBERT: Better take cover, they'll start any minute now.

CALDICOTT: Nasty jam, this . . . don't like the look of it.

CHARTERS: Got plenty of ammunition?

GILBERT: Whole pouch full.

CHARTERS: Good.

CALDICOTT: Duck down, you.

TODHUNTER: I'm not going to fight, it's madness.

MRS. TODHUNTER: It will be safer to protest down here.

We cut to a long shot of the SOLDIERS *by the cars.* GILBERT *is looking out of the window.*

GILBERT: Hallo, they're trying to work round to the other side.

TODHUNTER: You're behaving like a pack of fools . . . what chance have we got against a lot of armed men?

CALDICOTT: You heard what the Mother Superior said. If we surrender now, we're in for it.

The SOLDIERS *start coming towards the train, as* GILBERT *fires his gun. The window of the dining car is shattered by a* SOLDIER *firing from nearby the cars. He just misses* GILBERT *who is close to the window. There is a rapid exchange of cuts between the people in the dining car and the* SOLDIERS *outside.*

CALDICOTT: We'll never get to the match now.

MRS. TODHUNTER *off:* Give it to me . . . give it to me.

We cut to a shot of MR. *and* MRS. TODHUNTER *struggling.* CALDICOTT *comes on.*

CALDICOTT: What's going on here?

MRS. TODHUNTER: He's got a gun and he won't use it.

CALDICOTT: What's the idea?

TODHUNTER: I've told you, I won't be a party to this sort of thing. I don't believe in fighting.

CALDICOTT: Pacifist, eh? Won't work, old boy. Early

Christians tried it and got thrown to the lions. Come on, hand it over.

Another window in the dining car shatters.

MRS. TODHUNTER: I'm not afraid to use it.

CALDICOTT *off:* Probably more used to it. I once won a box of cigars.

CHARTERS: He's talking rot . . . he's a damned good shot.

CALDICOTT: Hope the old hand hasn't lost its cunning. You know, I'm half inclined to believe that there's some rational explanation to all this. Oh, rotten shot, only knocked his hat off.

He fires out of the train window.

MISS FROY: Would you mind if I talked to you for a minute?

GILBERT: What, now?

MISS FROY: Please forgive me, but it's very important.

GILBERT: Hang on to this for me, will you?

GILBERT *hands his gun to* CHARTERS.

CHARTERS: All right, I'll hold the fort.

MISS FROY: I think it's safer along here. You come too.

GILBERT: Keep your heads down.

They duck down together.

MISS FROY: I just wanted to tell you that I must be getting along now.

IRIS: But you can't, you'll never get away. You'll be shot down.

MISS FROY: I must take that risk. Listen carefully. In case I'm unlucky and you get through, I want you to take back a message to a Mr. Callendar at the Foreign Office at Whitehall.

IRIS: Then you are a spy.

MISS FROY: I always think that's such a grim word.

GILBERT: What is the message?

MISS FROY: It's a tune.

GILBERT: Tune?

MISS FROY: It contains, in code, of course, the vital clause of a secret pact between two European countries. I want you to memorise it.

GILBERT: Go ahead.

MISS FROY: The first part of it goes like this.

MISS FROY *starts to hum.*

MISS FROY: Oh, perhaps I'd better write it down. Have you got a piece of paper?

GILBERT: No, don't bother. I was brought up on music. I can memorise anything.

MISS FROY: Very well then.

She hums the rest of the tune.

CALDICOTT: Hello, the old girl's gone off her rocker.

TODHUNTER: I don't wonder. Why don't you face it? Those swines out there will go on firing till they kill the lot of us.

Pan to include MRS. TODHUNTER *and* CALDICOTT.

MRS. TODHUNTER: For goodness sake, shut up, Eric.

GILBERT *is now humming the tune.*

MISS FROY: That's right. Now we've got two chances instead of one.

GILBERT: You bet.

MISS FROY: You're sure you'll remember it?

GILBERT: Don't worry, I won't stop whistling it.

MISS FROY: I suppose this is my best way out?

GILBERT: Yes, just about.

IRIS: But you may be hit, and even if you do get away they'll stop you at the frontier. We can't let her go like this.

GILBERT: You know, this is a hell of a risk you're taking.

MISS FROY: In this sort of job one must take risks. I'm very grateful to you both for all you've done. I do hope and pray no harm will come to you, and that we shall all meet again . . . one day.

IRIS: I hope so too. Good luck.

GILBERT: Good luck.

MISS FROY: Will you help me out?

GILBERT: Yes, rather.

> GILBERT *helps* MISS FROY *out of a train window.*

GILBERT: Now take the weight . . . on top . . . right you are . . . I've got you.

IRIS: Goodbye.

> IRIS *and* GILBERT *watch as* MISS FROY *runs from the train.* DR. HARTZ *and the* SOLDIERS *see her go too. In the woods,* DR. HARTZ *shouts orders to his men.*

DR. HARTZ: Agrakan (Make sure of her).

> *There is a cut to a long shot of* MISS FROY *disappearing as seen by* GILBERT *and* IRIS.

IRIS: Was she hit?

GILBERT: I'm not sure.

> *As* DR. HARTZ *and the* SOLDIERS *look for* MISS FROY, CALDICOTT *fires the gun out of the window. We see a* SOLDIER *falling backwards.*

CALDICOTT: Well, that's the end of my twelve.

CHARTERS: There's not much left here, either.

GILBERT: We've only got one chance now. We've got to get this train going. Drive it back to the main line and then try and cross the frontier.

CALDICOTT: I say, that's a bit of a tall order, isn't it? Those driver fellows are not likely to do as you tell them, you know.

GILBERT *picks up the gun.*

GILBERT: We'll bluff them with this. Who's coming with me?

CALDICOTT: You can count on me.

CHARTERS: Me too.

GILBERT: We can't all go. You stay here and carry on, and if we have any luck we'll stop the train when we reach the points. And you jump out and switch them over.

CHARTERS *off:* Okay.

TODHUNTER: You idiots, you're just inviting death. I've had enough. Just because I've the sense to try and avoid being murdered, I'm accused of being a pacifist. All right, I'd rather be a rat than die like one. Think for a moment, will you? If we give ourselves up, they daren't murder us in cold blood. They're bound to give us a trial.

MRS. TODHUNTER: Stop jibbering, Eric. Nobody's listening to you.

TODHUNTER: Very well. You go your way, I'll go mine.

CHARTERS: Hey, where are you off to?

TODHUNTER: I know what I'm about. I'm doing the only sensible thing.

CHARTERS: Oh, let the fellow go if he wants to.

TODHUNTER *comes from the train carrying a white handkerchief. One of the* SOLDIERS *fires.* TODHUNTER *is hit and falls to the ground.*
GILBERT *and* CALDICOTT *climb onto the engine.*

MRS. TODHUNTER: Don't, please. Why aren't we going? Why aren't we going? They said we were going. Why aren't we?

IRIS: If only he can get us away now. He must!

CHARTERS: Only one left. I'll keep that for a sitter.

IRIS: They're moving away from the cars. They're coming towards us.

We see DR. HARTZ *and the* SOLDIERS *walking towards the train.*

CHARTERS: Pity we haven't a few more rounds.

MRS. TODHUNTER: It's funny. I told my husband when I left him that I wouldn't see him again.

IRIS: Gilbert! Gilbert!

DR. HARTZ *and the* SOLDIERS *continue walking towards the train.*

CHARTERS: By gad, we're off.

IRIS: This gives us a chance.

DR. HARTZ *and the* SOLDIERS, *seen from the windows, look on, as the train is moving away.*
Cut to the cab of the engine of the train. CALDICOTT, GILBERT *and two drivers are there.*

GILBERT: Come on, keep going.

One of the SOLDIERS *fires, an engine driver is hit. Now* DR. HARTZ *and his* SOLDIERS *begin following in a car. Another shot is fired. The second engine driver is hit by a bullet and falls from the train.*

CALDICOTT: I say, do you know how to control this thing?

GILBERT: I watched the fellow start it. Anyway, I know something about it. Once drove a miniature engine on the Dymchurch line.

CALDICOTT: Good. I'll look out for the points.

CALDICOTT *spots one of the cars following the train.* CHARTERS, *in the dining car, spots it too.*

CHARTERS: Blighters are chasing us. Look.

Everyone looks out of the window as we see a long shot of one of the pursuing cars.

IRIS: We can't have far to go.

There is a cut to the stunned OFFICER *regaining consciousness on the floor and seeing the revolver near him.*
There is a shot of the revolver as seen by the OFFICER, *and then another of the* OFFICER *himself, calculating his chances.*
Resume on CHARTERS, *and* IRIS *and* MRS. TODHUNTER.

CHARTERS: It's time for my little job changing the points. Thank heavens we shall be in neutral territory.

The OFFICER *rises with the revolver.*

OFFICER: That will not be necessary. I'm sorry, but the points, as you call them, will not be changed over. Please be seated.

Cut back to the cab of the engine, where CALDICOTT, *acting as look out, spots the points ahead.*

CALDICOTT: There they are, just ahead of us. Do you think you can stop it?

GILBERT: Hope so.

In the dining car, the OFFICER *brandishes the gun in front of the others. The* NUN *is behind the* OFFICER.

OFFICER: You'll keep quite still until my friends arrive. If anyone moves, I'm afraid I shall have to shoot.

IRIS: There's just one thing you don't know, Captain. There's only one bullet left in that gun, and if you shoot me . . . you'll give the others a chance. You're in rather a difficult position, aren't you?

OFFICER: Sit down, please.

The OFFICER *is preoccupied with* IRIS *talking.* CHARTERS *moves in to block the* OFFICER'S *view as the* NUN *leaves.*

IRIS: All right.

The train stops close to the points. In the engine, CALDICOTT *and* GILBERT *look worried.*

CALDICOTT: Where the devil's Charters?

The NUN *jumps from the train and goes to the points junction and moves the points.*
SOLDIERS *in the car commence firing as the* NUN *runs back towards the train.*

CALDICOTT: Go ahead, she's done it.

The NUN *runs to the cab of the engine as* GILBERT *prepares to ease the brake.* GILBERT *and* CALDICOTT *help her aboard the engine.*

NUN: Ouch! It's all right, it's just my legs.

On the road, a second car is arriving. The BARONESS *alights from it, just in time to watch the train crossing the border. Pan to include* DR. HARTZ.

BARONESS: Barogluts farshadram (They've got away after all).

DR. HARTZ: Car marniblon. Or as they say in English, jolly good luck to them.

GILBERT, CALDICOTT *and the* NUN *are delighted.*

CALDICOTT: My word, I'm glad all that's over, aren't you? Heaven knows what the Government will say about all this.

GILBERT: Nothing at all. They'll hush it up.

CALDICOTT: What?

GILBERT: Hey, take your hand off that thing. I've got to remember a tune.

CALDICOTT: Remember . . .

Dissolve to a Channel steamer, then to a train drawing into Victoria Railway Station.
Cut to IRIS *and* GILBERT *in a compartment of the train.*

ATTENDANT: Porter, sir?

GILBERT: No, thanks.

IRIS: Well, we're home, Gilbert. Can't you stop humming that awful tune? You must know it backwards.

GILBERT: Oh, I'm not taking any risks. Will Charles be here to meet you?

IRIS: I expect so.

GILBERT: Well, you'll be pretty busy between now and Thursday.

IRIS: I could meet you for lunch or dinner, if you'd like it.

GILBERT: Sorry, I didn't mean that. Oh, as a matter of fact, I've got to deliver this theme song to Miss Froy, and when I've done that, I'm going to dash up to Yorkshire and finish my book.

IRIS: Oh, I see.

GILBERT: Ready?

IRIS: Yes.

IRIS *and* GILBERT *walk along the platform among other passengers.* CHARTERS *and* CALDICOTT *are just ahead of them.*

CHARTERS: Ample time to catch the six-fifty to Manchester after all.

They pass a newspaper stand and notice a newsvendor carrying a poster which reads:
TEST MATCH
ABANDONED:

FLOODS
LATE EVENING
EXTRA NEWS

CALDICOTT *and* CHARTERS *are speechless.*

GILBERT: Any sign of Charles yet?

IRIS: No, I can't see him.

GILBERT: Well, this is where we say goodbye.

IRIS *suddenly see* CHARLES *and dives into a taxi.*

GILBERT: What's the matter?

From the point of view of IRIS *and* GILBERT, *we see* CHARLES. *He is too appallingly civilised.*

GILBERT: Charles?

IRIS: Yes, you heartless, callous, selfish, swollen-headed beast, you.

GILBERT *kisses* IRIS, *who kisses him back.*

TAXI DRIVER: Are you going anywhere?

GILBERT *and* IRIS *stop kissing each other.*

GILBERT: Foreign Office.

Dissolve to the interior lobby of the Foreign Office where GILBERT *and* IRIS *are waiting together.*

IRIS: Where are we going for our honeymoon?

GILBERT: I don't know. Somewhere quiet. Somewhere where there are no trains.

A MAN *enters in the background.*

MAN: Mr. Callendar will see you now.

GILBERT: Wait a minute. It's gone!

IRIS: What's gone?

GILBERT: The tune. I've forgotten it!

IRIS: No. Oh, no!

GILBERT: Wait a minute, let me concentrate.

GILBERT *starts to hum.*

IRIS: No, no, no, no, that's the Wedding March.

GILBERT: This is awful. I've done nothing else but sing it since the day before yesterday, and . . . and now I've forgotten it completely.

A piano is heard playing the tune. **Track forward with** GILBERT *and* IRIS *into* CALLENDAR'S *room to reveal* MISS FROY *seated at the piano.*

IRIS: Miss Froy!

GILBERT: Well, I'll be hanged.

Fade out to THE END.